Cambridge Elements

Elements in Public Policy
edited by
M. Ramesh
National University of Singapore (NUS)
Michael Howlett
Simon Fraser University, British Columbia
Xun WU
Hong Kong University of Science and Technology (Guangzhou)
Judith Clifton
University of Cantabria
Eduardo Araral
National University of Singapore (NUS)

TAXATION AND SOCIAL POLICY

Financing the Welfare State

Michal Koreh
University of Haifa

Olivier Jacques
University of Montreal

Daniel Béland
McGill University

CAMBRIDGE
UNIVERSITY PRESS

Shaftesbury Road, Cambridge CB2 8EA, United Kingdom

One Liberty Plaza, 20th Floor, New York, NY 10006, USA

477 Williamstown Road, Port Melbourne, VIC 3207, Australia

314–321, 3rd Floor, Plot 3, Splendor Forum, Jasola District Centre,
New Delhi – 110025, India

Cambridge University Press is part of Cambridge University Press & Assessment,
a department of the University of Cambridge.

We share the University's mission to contribute to society through the pursuit of
education, learning and research at the highest international levels of excellence.

www.cambridge.org
Information on this title: www.cambridge.org/9781009565707

DOI: 10.1017/9781009446990

© Michal Koreh, Olivier Jacques and Daniel Béland 2026

This publication is in copyright. Subject to statutory exception and to the provisions of relevant collective licensing agreements, with the exception of the Creative Commons version the link for which is provided below,no reproduction of any part may take place without the written permission of Cambridge University Press & Assessment.

An online version of this work is published at doi.org/10.1017/9781009446990 under a Creative Commons Open Access license CC-BY-NC-ND 4.0 which permits re-use, distribution and reproduction in any medium for non-commercial purposes providing appropriate credit to the original work is given. You may not distribute derivative works without permission. To view a copy of this license, visit https://creativecommons.org/licenses/by-nc-nd/4.0

When citing this work, please include a reference to the DOI 10.1017/9781009446990

First published 2026

A catalogue record for this publication is available from the British Library

A Cataloging-in-Publication data record for this Element is available from the Library of Congress

ISBN 978-1-009-56570-7 Hardback
ISBN 978-1-009-44698-3 Paperback
ISSN 2398-4058 (online)
ISSN 2514-3565 (print)

Cambridge University Press & Assessment has no responsibility for the persistence or accuracy of URLs for external or third-party internet websites referred to in this publication and does not guarantee that any content on such websites is, or will remain, accurate or appropriate.

For EU product safety concerns, contact us at Calle de José Abascal, 56, 1°, 28003 Madrid, Spain, or email eugpsr@cambridge.org

Taxation and Social Policy

Financing the Welfare State

Elements in Public Policy

DOI: 10.1017/9781009446990
First published online: April 2026

Michal Koreh
University of Haifa

Olivier Jacques
University of Montreal

Daniel Béland
McGill University

Author for correspondence: Michal Koreh, mkoreh@univ.haifa.ac.il

Abstract: This Element maps the relationship between taxation and social policy from a comparative and historical perspective. It critically reviews studies in fiscal sociology, history, political science, and political economy to highlight blind spots in the body of knowledge that future studies could explore. It shows that studying the revenue side of social policy offers compelling answers to central questions tackled in welfare state scholarship and addresses questions such as: What explains the introduction and timing of social programs? How can we understand processes of welfare state expansion and retrenchment? What determines the redistributive capacity of welfare states? What accounts for variations in redistributive capacity between groups and across generations in different countries? While bringing in the financing side of social policy complements prevailing accounts in the welfare state literature, studying financing can also transform how we understand social policy. This title is also available as Open Access on Cambridge Core.

Keywords: taxation, social policy, welfare state, financing, public finance

© Michal Koreh, Olivier Jacques and Daniel Béland 2026

ISBNs: 9781009565707 (HB), 9781009446983 (PB), 9781009446990 (OC)
ISSNs: 2398-4058 (online), 2514-3565 (print)

Contents

1 Introduction 1

2 The Architecture of Welfare State Financing 3

3 How Do Fiscal Development and Welfare State Development Relate? 19

4 Fiscal Foundations of Welfare State Diversity 38

5 Public Opinion on Taxation 50

6 Conclusion 62

References 65

1 Introduction

Taxation is central to public policy, as it underpins all functions of modern states. It is particularly crucial for social policy, which "is concerned with the ways societies across the world meet human needs for security, education, work, health and wellbeing" (Platt, 2021). Tasks within the umbrella of social policy constitute the largest component of public spending in affluent democracies. Karl Marx (1978) identified taxes as the state's "source of life," while Joseph Schumpeter and Rudolf Goldscheid, the founders of fiscal sociology, recognized the study of taxation as a crucial gateway for gaining insight into the development of states and state–society relations (Martin et al., 2009). Schumpeter (1991 [1918]) argued that tax policy is both a "symptom" and a "cause" of large-scale changes in the economy and society (Swedberg, 1991: 48). By examining taxation alongside spending, we access what Goldscheid (1917/1958) termed "the skeleton of the state stripped of all misleading ideologies" (quoted in Swedberg, 1991: 48). Like a skeleton, a state's fiscal structure reveals its fundamental priorities and power dynamics.

Despite the foundational role of taxation in social policy, welfare state scholarship has long focused more on the spending side of welfare states than on their revenue sources (Campbell, 1993; Koreh and Béland, 2017; Martin et al., 2009; Morgan and Prasad, 2009; Ruane, Collins and Sinfield, 2020).

Although research on welfare state financing has significantly expanded, addressing both tax and non-tax funding mechanisms, its emphasis has primarily been on how financing reflects broader welfare state politics. Using Schumpeter's terminology, much of this literature has highlighted the *symptomatic* significance of welfare finance but has yet to fully develop its *causal* role in shaping welfare state development.

Welfare state financing is symptomatic in the sense that the ways countries finance their social policies offer insights into the kinds of social contracts underpinning national social protection systems, reflecting diverse redistributive ambitions, conceptions of solidarity, and legitimacy among societies (Morel and Palme, 2018; Sjoberg, 2000). However, state financing – including that of welfare programmes – is not only a reflection of social policy preferences. It is also driven by broader political and economic imperatives such as war, economic crises, and geopolitical shifts, which shape the institutions and policies through which social protection is financed (Genschel and Seelkopf, 2021). Financing choices, whether symptomatic of welfare state politics or of broader political and economic forces, actively shape the politics and execution of welfare programmes. The combination of the force of law with the power of economic incentives that is inherent to taxation and other mandatory financing methods makes welfare state financing a powerful driver of social and political behaviour, directly influencing welfare politics, policies, and outcomes. Moreover, taxation remains a site of ongoing tension between state and society where the obligations of citizens and the responsibilities of the state are continually redefined (Martin et al., 2009).

While scholarship on welfare financing has expanded, it remains predominantly benefit-centred, treating financing as a reflection of the politics of the welfare state (for a critique, see Koreh & Béland, 2017). Explanations often assume that conflicts over welfare generosity and programme structure determine struggles over how the financial burden of social protection is distributed. As a result, financing is framed as an outcome – an extension of political preferences regarding benefits – rather than as an independent factor that shapes social policy. This perspective narrows the analytical scope of welfare state research, reinforcing the notion that financing merely mirrors distributive struggles rather than influencing the fundamental design and trajectory of welfare states.

When scholars do consider the causal role of welfare financing, they often reduce it to its impact on resource availability (Koreh & Béland, 2017). In this literature, the fiscal side of social policy matters primarily because it determines the possible scope of social spending. Resource abundance is seen as facilitating social spending and welfare state expansion, while resource scarcity is understood to create conditions for expenditure constraints and retrenchment (Kato, 2003; Pierson, 1994). This perspective is evident in studies on welfare state retrenchment, which highlight how shifting fiscal circumstances – whether due to economic stagnation, rising welfare costs, or revenue-reducing tax policies – have increased fiscal pressures on the state and, consequently, shaped welfare politics (Pierson, 1996, 2001; Steuerle, 1996).

While these perspectives capture important dynamics, they overlook the additional ways in which financing structures and financing politics shape welfare states. The way states finance social protection – how they pool risks, raise revenue, and structure economic activity – is inseparable from how they fund other state functions. Just as welfare state politics influences financing debates, financing structures also shape welfare state design, affecting not only the distribution of costs but also the form, character, and political dynamics of social protection.

In this Cambridge Element, we bring together key literature streams from fiscal sociology, political science, history, and the political economy of taxation, alongside welfare state research, to provide a comprehensive mapping of the relationship between taxation and social policy from a comparative and historical perspective. As the different sections of this Element demonstrate, these diverse literatures reveal that, beyond simply influencing resource availability, fiscal structures and politics play a central role in explaining the introduction of social programmes and its timing (Koreh, 2017; Leff, 1983), the comparative differences in the structure of social protection (Estevez-Abe, 2001; Manow, 2010; Schmitt et al., 2020), variations in redistributive capacities (Guillaud et al., 2020; Jacques & Noël, 2018; Prasad & Deng, 2009), and the forces driving or impeding welfare state expansion and retrenchment (Koreh, 2017; Manow & Seils, 2000; Palier, 2010). This short book suggests that, while the inclusion of the financing side of social policy complements existing accounts, it also offers new insights that can transform how we understand social policy.

Section 2 introduces the complex architecture of welfare state financing, detailing the diverse array of instruments modern states use to fund social programmes. More specifically, it analyses how different tax instruments – such as social insurance contribution (SIC), value added tax (VAT), tax expenditure, and private financing – shape political dynamics and influence the design of social protection systems. Section 3 explores the historical relationship between fiscal development and welfare state development. It examines how contingent events, socio-economic processes, and the interplay of political and institutional factors shape the development of fiscal systems and welfare states. Section 4 maps the comparative differences in tax structures across countries. It explains how these design differences reinforce the institutional character and redistributive outcomes of different welfare state regimes, while identifying the factors that cause tax regimes to diverge. Section 5 discusses public opinion dynamics regarding taxation by analysing the main individual and contextual determinants of preferences for tax levels and progressivity. This section also discusses how public opinion shapes the politics of tax reforms. Section 6 offers concluding remarks leading to the formulation of a brief agenda for future research that stresses the need to bridge the literature on the Global North discussed in this Cambridge Element with the scholarship about, and the empirical realities of, the Global South.

2 The Architecture of Welfare State Financing

Modern tax systems are diverse and welfare state financing systems are even more varied, relying on both tax and non-tax instruments. The variety of instruments and revenue governance structures, coupled with their causal significance, underscore the centrality of the financing side in the analysis of differences between welfare states and of their development over time.

Welfare state financing systems consist of two distinct groups of policy instruments. The first group comprises *revenue-generating instruments* that create the resources with which welfare state benefits and services are financed. The second group comprises *tax expenditure instruments* representing an indirect form of welfare spending that Christopher Howard (1997) termed the "hidden welfare state." This concept suggests that there is a hidden aspect to the welfare state where individuals' and families' social provisions are subsidized through forgone tax revenues. Following these two groups of policy instruments, the upcoming section addresses the administration of welfare state financing, another essential component of tax systems responsible for assessing, collecting, and managing revenues. Each of these instruments and governance structures, as well as the interaction between them, have far-reaching implications for the politics, characteristics, and outcomes of social policy.

2.1 Revenue-Generating Instruments

Revenue-generating instruments represent the financial mechanisms through which social welfare systems are funded, embodying the complex intersection of economic policy, social redistribution, and state–society relations. These instruments are not merely technical financial tools, but deeply political mechanisms that reflect and help reproduce social contracts, distributional preferences, and broader institutional arrangements. Revenue-generating instruments differ along at least six dimensions: (1) their public–private nature, (2) their tax base (what and who is being taxed), (3) their link to income (being progressive, regressive, or proportional), (4) their link to benefits (having a requited or unrequited nature), (5) their funding mechanism (being fully funded, partially funded, or pay-as-you-go (PAYGO)), and (6) their visibility.

The "Public–Private" Dimension – Social programmes can be publicly financed through various tax methods that are legally obligatory, such as the personal income tax (PIT), consumption tax (like VAT), and SIC.[1] Yet, social programmes can also be financed through individualized forms of financing derived from private or occupational payments. While such payments can be voluntary, they can also be obligatory, as is the case when states require workers and or employers to contribute to individual private pension funds or when a private co-pay is required when utilizing a public programme. As the review in Section 2.1 demonstrates, the reliance on public or private forms of financing has far-reaching implications for welfare entitlements, programme coverage, characteristics, and the state's redistributive capacity (Schmitt et al., 2020).

---

[1] These three public instruments (PIT, VAT, and SIC) are considered the central public sources of welfare state financing. Along with private modes of finance, they are the primary focus of this review. However, they are not the only tax types. Other significant tax methods, such as corporate income taxes (CIT), property taxes, excise taxes, and inheritance taxes, also contribute to the overall revenue pool for funding social welfare programs.

The "Tax Base" Dimension – refers to the economic activities and assets that form the basis for applying the tax rate and determining the tax liability of individuals, businesses, or other entities. Different tax methods vary in their respective tax base. For example, in the case of PIT, the tax base typically comprises the overall income earned by an individual, encompassing wages, business profits, capital gains, and other income sources. In contrast, SIC applies exclusively to wages. Meanwhile, the tax base for VAT is determined by the total value of goods and services sold.

Two aspects of the tax base bear implications for the revenue generation capacity of welfare states: its broadness and its impact on economic performance. A broader tax base allows even small changes in rates to generate substantial revenue increases, unlike narrower tax bases. Among major tax instruments, VAT is potentially the most socially inclusive, as it covers not only the formal sector but also some input purchases by the informal sector (i.e., unregistered economic activities operating outside government regulation). In contrast, the tax base of PIT is limited to income earners in the formal economy (i.e., economic activities that are registered, regulated, and taxed by the government), entirely excluding the informal sector (Genschel and Seelkopf, 2021; Wagner, 2012). The breadth of the tax base is also influenced by policies that create exemptions, loopholes, and thresholds, all of which can shape the overall scope of taxable activities.

The tax base also influences revenue generation potential through its impact on economic performance. The taxation of certain economic bases is argued to have fewer distorting effects, making them more conducive to economic growth and thus entailing a larger revenue potential (Prasad & Deng, 2009). Similarly, some activities are less mobile than others, rendering them less vulnerable, under conditions of globalization, to tax competition pressures (Genschel & Schwarz, 2011). Consumption taxes, argued to possess these two traits, feature a broad base that facilitates the development of large welfare states. Simultaneously, their reliance on consumption, a less mobile economic activity, insulates them from the pressures of globalization in contrast to, for instance, corporate taxes (Genschel, 2002; Morgan and Prasad, 2009). To the contrary, several studies have argued that social policy funding by social security contributions pose an economic risk, as it increases labour costs and reduces firms' competitiveness (Kemmerling, 2009).

The "Link to Income" Dimension – refers to how individual payments relate to income, manifesting in progressive, regressive, or proportional tax structures. In a progressive system, tax rates rise with income, reducing income inequality. Regressive taxes, however, place a disproportionate burden on lower-income earners by applying lower rates as incomes increase. Proportional taxes maintain a constant rate regardless of income, preserving existing income inequalities.

Different tax instruments create varying links to income and in turn impact redistribution. PIT is typically progressive, taxing higher incomes at higher rates, thereby decreasing income gaps after taxation. Conversely, VAT tends to be regressive, as it applies a uniform rate that burdens lower-income individuals more heavily relative to their earnings, thus widening income gaps. Social insurance contribution, usually seen as proportional, is neutral in distributive terms, because everyone contributes the same percentage of their income. However, when there's a ceiling on insurable income, higher earners pay a lower effective rate, introducing regressive redistribution (Genschel, 2002).

While some tax instruments may be regressive, private financing mechanisms tend to be even more so (Koreh et al., 2024). For example, private health insurance premiums are lump sums based on coverage and individual risk, rather than income, causing higher-income individuals to pay a smaller share of their earnings compared to lower-income ones. However, it should be emphasized that the redistributive outcomes of tax systems are not determined by structure alone but depend significantly on tax levels – the total tax revenue as a percentage of GDP (Guillaud et al., 2020). Though progressivity enhances redistribution at any given revenue level, countries with lower overall tax levels, even if they have progressive systems, may only see limited redistributive outcomes. In fact, research shows a negative correlation between tax progressivity and tax levels, indicating that more progressive systems often generate less revenue, which in turn limits their capacity to reduce income inequality (Guillaud et al., 2020; Steinmo, 1993). We further discuss this stylized fact in Section 4.

The "Link to Benefits" Dimension – examines the connection between payments and receipts in welfare provisions across different tax instruments. This link ranges from "requited" (where there is a direct relation between what you pay and what you receive) to "unrequited" (where there is no direct correlation). Private financing instruments, such as out-of-pocket payments and private insurance premiums, are highly requited in the sense that individual payments reflect service prices, coverage, and risk profiles. At the opposite end, general taxation instruments, such as PIT, or VAT, are unrequited and taxpayers cannot expect specific benefits in return (Martin et al., 2009).

Between these ends, hybrid forms exist. For example, SICs operate on a partially requited basis, but the connection between payments and receipt is weaker than in private financing and can vary in strength (Campbell and Morgan, 2005; Kemmerling, 2021; Wagner, 2012). In weaker forms, benefit eligibility of a SIC relies on a contribution record, but benefits themselves are uniform and unrelated to individual contributions. In contrast, under stronger linkages, contributions correlate with entitlement levels, underpinning the income-related nature of many social insurance programmes (Clasen, 2001).

These variations in the link between payments and benefits have significant consequences for social protection characteristics, impacting programme coverage and eligibility criteria (Cichon et al., 2004; Manow, 2010; Morel & Palme, 2018). Contribution-financed programmes typically cover only wage earners in the formal economy who pay into the system. Where contribution levels are linked to entitlement levels, these programmes maintain a status-preserving function, allowing beneficiaries to sustain their standard of living during periods of unemployment or incapacity to work (Clasen, 2001; Esping-Andersen, 1990).

In contrast, tax-financed social protection, which is unrequited, can adopt different forms of coverage. It may provide universal benefits based on citizenship, as seen in many Nordic welfare models, where all citizens receive protection regardless of their tax contributions. Alternatively, it can be means-tested, targeting the very poor, as in Anglo-American welfare systems. In these cases, eligibility is generally conditioned on income levels, excluding those who contribute but exceed the income threshold.

These differences have also important redistributive implications affecting the state's ability to reduce inequality (Schmitt et al., 2020). The closer the link between payments and receipts, the less scope there is for redistribution. Out-of-pocket payments provide no redistribution, as individuals pay directly for services without any risk pooling. Private insurance, while offering some degree of risk pooling, still limits redistribution, because premiums are tied to individual risk profiles and coverage levels.

Social insurance contributions offer greater redistributive potential, particularly when contributions are linked to salary rather than set at a flat rate. This structure ensures that individuals contribute based on their ability to pay. In contrast, universal tax-financed programmes provide broad coverage and significant redistribution by spreading the cost across the population, including those who don't directly benefit. At the highest end of redistributive potential sit means-tested, tax-financed programmes, which target resources specifically toward those with the lowest incomes while being funded by higher earners.

However, just like tax systems, redistributive outcomes in social protection depend not only on the structure of tax–benefit linkages but also on the size of the redistributive pool (i.e., both the taxes collected and the spending levels). Political factors, such as the legitimacy of the welfare state and the willingness to pay taxes, play a key role here. In their well-known work on the paradox of redistribution, Korpi and Palme (1998) argue that overall redistribution tends to be higher in systems where contributors, through either social insurance or universal structures, can expect to benefit from the system themselves. In contrast, strictly targeted, means-tested systems, despite being the most progressive in structure, often result in limited overall redistribution due to a smaller resource pool, leading to higher poverty and inequality rates. This insight has been confirmed by more recent studies (Brady and Bostic, 2015; Jacques and Noël, 2018).

The "Funding Mechanism" Dimension – refers to the methods through which financial resources are accumulated and utilized to cover the costs of social programmes throughout their life cycle. This dimension reflects critical intertemporal choices regarding cost allocation between present and future, taking three primary forms: PAYGO, fully funded, or semi-funded approaches (Cichon et al., 2004; on intertemporal choices see Jacobs, 2011).

Private financing instruments, such as insurance premiums for private health insurance or contributions to private pension accounts, are typically fully funded. In a fully funded system, current contributions not only cover immediate expenses but also accumulate sufficient assets to fully cover future liabilities. For example, in a fully funded pension account, the fund's total assets at any time are required to match its projected future obligations. In contrast, general taxation methods follow a PAYGO approach, where present tax revenues are used to cover current spending without creating a dedicated reserve. A tax-based pension scheme, for instance, uses current budget allocations to fund ongoing benefits.

Social insurance programmes typically employ a semi-funded method, which falls between these two approaches. In this model, a reserve is built up, but it does not cover all future liabilities. Instead, it serves two primary purposes: mitigating the frequency of contribution increases and providing a financial buffer during economic downturns.

The distinction between these financing methods is particularly significant in the debate over pension systems and their ability to cope with demographic aging. Advocates of fully funded pension systems argue that they are better equipped to handle aging populations because each generation accumulates the necessary funds to finance its own retirement. In this view, even if the ratio of workers to retirees declines, retirees will have pre-funded their benefits, preventing an increased burden on younger cohorts. This argument gained traction in the 1990s and 2000s, prompting pension reforms that shifted from PAYGO to funded models (Orenstein, 2013).

Yet, this perspective remains contested. As Barr (2002) and others have argued, from a macroeconomic standpoint, funded systems do not inherently offer a clear advantage over PAYGO. The core issue is not whether pensions are funded or PAYGO but how demographic aging affects future output. Even if retirees accumulate financial assets, they still require goods and services produced by the working population. A shrinking workforce, therefore, constrains an economy's ability to meet these demands, regardless of the financing model (Morel and Palme, 2018). Thus, demographic aging presents fundamental challenges to pension sustainability across all funding structures.

At the same time, both models face distinct vulnerabilities. While fully funded systems are exposed to financial market risks – such as volatility, inflation, and economic downturns that can erode accumulated assets – PAYGO programmes rely on future governments' political will, making them susceptible to shifting fiscal priorities.

This underscores why the fiscal sustainability of pension systems cannot be assessed solely based on their funding mechanism. Sustainability depends on broader factors, including economic growth, labour market dynamics, and political choices regarding benefit levels and contributions. While fully funded systems may alleviate immediate fiscal pressures on the working-age population, they are not immune to structural economic risks. Conversely, despite their reliance on intergenerational transfers, PAYGO systems offer built-in flexibility to adjust benefits and contributions in response to economic and demographic shifts.

Beyond pensions, funding mechanisms shape the financial capacity of social programmes more broadly. Fully and semi-funded approaches transform social programmes from mere expenditure mechanisms into potential capital generators. By accumulating and investing funds, these mechanisms generate additional resources through interest earnings and investment returns, thereby expanding the programmes' spending capacity (Jacobs, 2011).

The choice of funding methods also influences political dynamics. Pay-as-you-go systems typically focus political debates narrowly on benefit levels and contribution rates. In contrast, fully and semi-funded programmes introduce additional complexities, as the accumulation and investment of programme assets can serve additional societal objectives – such as industrial policy, government debt financing, or financial market development (Estevez-Abe, 2001; Kangas, 2009; Musgrave & Musgrave, 1973; Park, 2011).

Moreover, in fully and semi-funded systems, the investment component reshapes political constituencies and fosters new interest groups. Stakeholders' concerns extend beyond traditional welfare considerations to include the management, and strategic deployment of programme funds, generating new power struggles and policy trade-offs (Hassel et al., 2019; Koreh & Béland, 2017). As further elaborated in Section 3, these broader political interests play a crucial role in shaping the adoption, design, and evolution of social policies.

The "Tax Visibility" Dimension – refers to how noticeable or transparent the tax imposition is to individuals. Visibility encompasses the clarity and awareness that taxpayers have regarding the taxes they are required to pay. Scholars argue that different tax instruments vary in their visibility and that direct taxes, like PIT, tend to be more visible than indirect taxes, such as VAT (Martin, 2015; Steuerle, 1992). This is because individuals directly see the amount deducted from their income when paying income taxes, making the tax obligation more apparent. In contrast, the VAT is included in the price of goods and services, making it less noticeable to consumers. Social insurance contributions are deducted from wages but are seen as less visible than income taxes because employers typically pay a portion of them. While scholars argue that both employers' and employees' contributions impact net income (Palme et al., 2009), workers generally perceive only their direct deductions as costs. Even when employer contributions appear on pay checks, they are not always seen as affecting take-home pay, making SICs seem like a lower-cost way to fund benefits compared to more visible direct taxes.

Such visibility differences have influenced welfare state politics and state revenue capacity. Visible taxes are seen to provoke greater opposition, often leading to tax revolts and backlash, whereas invisible taxes are associated with greater tax consent and, consequently, a higher capacity for states to raise revenues and finance generous welfare states (Campbell & Morgan, 2005; Martin & Gabay, 2018; Steuerle, 1992; Wilensky, 2002). However, as discussed in Section 5, there are relatively few studies of public opinion of different taxes and the visibility argument is not always confirmed by empirical studies.

This brief review highlights the distinct characteristics of revenue-generating instruments and the trade-offs they entail. Value added tax, being broad based, regressive, and low visibility, is an efficient revenue-raising tool often dubbed a "money machine." However, its regressive nature means it disproportionately burdens low-income earners. In contrast, PIT, with its progressive structure, often exempts lower incomes, alleviating their tax burden. Despite this, its high visibility and unrequited nature make it politically sensitive, often sparking resistance that constrains its use for mass revenue generation.

Social insurance contributions, characterized by their requited nature and lower visibility, provide broader coverage and political acceptability, though they often exclude non-workers and, in some cases, low-earning or part-time workers, leaving some individuals without social protection. Private financing mechanisms, like individualized pension contributions or private health insurance, are highly requited and regressive, and while they may exacerbate inequality, they remain crucial in countries with weaker state capacity for providing essential social services (Schmitt et al., 2020). These varying features underscore not only the centrality of welfare state financing instruments in shaping social policy but also identifies the inherent political and fiscal challenges in designing comprehensive welfare state financing systems.

2.2 Tax Expenditures

Tax expenditures are policy instruments that intersect directly with welfare state financing, as they point to how the state can forgo tax revenues to advance social policy objectives. From this perspective, as Adrian Sinfield (2023) explains, tax expenditures overlap with what Richard Titmuss (2019) called "fiscal welfare," a form of social policy delivery distinct from "social welfare" (public social benefits and services) and "occupational welfare" (benefits tied to employment status). This perspective has long informed the comparative study of social policy, with a focus on the "changing boundaries of the welfare state" (Flora and Heidenheimer, 1981), and it remains influential today (Morel, 2025; Pavolini et al., 2024; Sinfield, 2020). As for the concept of tax expenditures, which "mirrors the term *public expenditures* to show spending policies being run through the tax system" (Sinfield, 2023: 46), it was developed by economist Stanley S. Surrey (1973), who published a major book on the topic focusing on the United States more than half a century ago.

Tax expenditure instruments encompass exemptions, deductions, allowances, or credits targeted at specific groups or "social" activities (Morel and Palme, 2018). Tax expenditures subsidize and incentivize private welfare provisions such as pension savings, housing, healthcare, and childcare expenses. The OECD calls them "tax breaks with a social purpose" (Adema et al., 2011). Despite not involving direct monetary transfers like cash benefits, tax expenditures constitute an indirect form of spending through foregone revenues (Howard, 1997), making them a crucial element in welfare provision.

When we turn to the recent, in-depth, political and policy analysis of tax expenditures, much has been written on the topic in the United States (Bellafiore, 2018; Burman et al., 2008; Faricy and Ellis, 2014; Hacker, 2002; Howard, 1997; Mettler, 2011). For instance, in the widely cited book *The Hidden Welfare State*, Christopher Howard (1997) reminds us that tax expenditures in general "can take the form of tax deductions, tax credits, preferential tax rates, tax deferrals, or outright exclusion of income from taxation. They subsidize a broad range of activities, from oil exploration to the rehabilitation of historic buildings" (3). In his book, Howard (1997) documents the expansion of social policy-related tax expenditures in the United States.

The four policy areas studied systematically in the book point to the diversity of tax expenditures, which can belong to different areas of the welfare state such as housing, pension, and employment policies, including home mortgage interest deduction aimed at fostering home ownership, "favorable tax treatment of employer-provided retirement pensions" (Howard, 1997: 48), the Earned Income Tax Credit for low-income workers, and the Targeted Jobs Tax Credit for members of vulnerable populations seeking employment. As Howard (1997: 24) shows, these four examples are only the tip of the tax expenditure iceberg in the United States, as the use of the tax system to promote social policy is both widespread and diverse in nature and scope.

Massive and fragmented, the "hidden welfare state" has a clearly regressive effect. This is the case partly because subsidizing employers to encourage them to offer health insurance and pension coverage to their workers means that "more affluent citizens are the main beneficiaries of the hidden welfare state. As a general rule, these benefits are most likely to be available to workers in larger companies, unionized industries, and better-paying occupations" (31). In this context, Howard (1997) claims that the "hidden welfare state" has redistributive patterns that are distinct from the "visible welfare state."

Finally, partly because of this, the politics surrounding the "hidden welfare state" are distinct in nature, leading to the argument that "the differences between direct expenditures and tax expenditures as policy tools affect the nature of political support for each type of spending" (12). Yet, the politics surrounding the "hidden welfare state" varies greatly from one policy tool to the next, something that reflects the internal fragmentation of this welfare state (Howard, 1997).

The findings from Howard's book were widely influential, encouraging other scholars to directly consider tax expenditures in the analysis of social policy in the United States. For instance, Jacob Hacker (Hacker, 2002; Hacker, 2004) stresses the importance of tax expenditures in the development and politics of voluntary private health insurance and pension benefits in the United States. His 2002 book, *The Divided Welfare State*, draws on the work of Howard (1997) and points to the importance of tax expenditures aimed at stimulating the development of private health insurance and pensions in the United States: "the two largest expenditures in the federal code are the exclusions of employer-sponsored health insurance and employer pension contributions and plan earnings from taxable income – which together reduce annual federal revenues by nearly $200 billion, about what is spent on Medicare" (11). The broader analysis discusses the role of tax expenditures within the politics of private social policy in the United States. In that sense, his work is close to Jennifer Klein's (2004) historical analysis of the rise of private health insurance and pension benefits in that country.

Even more than Hacker's book, Suzanne Mettler's 2011 *The Submerged State: How Invisible Government Policies Undermine American Democracy* stresses the importance of paying close attention to the "hidden welfare state" (Howard, 1997) in the United States. A student of public opinion and public policy, Mettler (2011) stresses the negative impact of "invisible" policies, such as tax expenditures on US democracy, as they make citizens largely unaware of key public actions that affect their lives profoundly. Turning to early fiscal and social policy reforms enacted towards the beginning of the Obama administration (2009–17), she argues that the lack of awareness of these policies on the part of citizens fostered political discontent and contributed to the rise of the Tea Party movement.

While not focusing exclusively on tax expenditures, Mettler's book *The Submerged State* (2011) does locate them in a broader conversation about democracy and social policy in the United States that explicitly builds on the work of Howard (1997) and his followers. For her, the "submerged state" and the tax expenditures featured in it are the product of an ongoing conservative restructuring of US social policy that favours narrow economic interests at the expense of the majority of citizens, who remain largely unaware of costly policies affecting them indirectly. In fact, the more a welfare state relies on "hidden" or "submerged" tax expenditures, the less importance voters put on social policy issues (Gingrich, 2014).

This scholarship suggests that reliance on tax expenditures is not merely a technical debate between indirect over direct spending instruments but has instead distinct distributional and political outcomes. Tax expenditures typically favour middle- and upper-middle-income groups (Howard, 1997) and encourage the development of private welfare markets, which also tend to benefit these groups (Morgan, 2005). Moreover, due to the oft-hidden nature of state provisions, dependence on tax expenditures affects welfare state politics and legitimacy (Hacker, 2002; Martin et al., 2009).

The public opinion implications of tax expenditures are explored systematically in *The Other Side of the Coin: Public Opinion toward Social Tax Expenditures*. In this recent book, Faricy and Ellis (2021) "find not only that social tax expenditures are generally popular, but that these programs are supported by subpopulations that normally are not inclined to favor public social spending" (13). They find tax expenditures are popular for three reasons: "a policy design's appeal to citizens who favor limited government, its interference with attempts to politicize and racialize beneficiaries, and its signals to citizens about the deservingness of program beneficiaries" (9). In this context, there is broad public support for social tax expenditures in the United States. For Ellis and Faricy, this situation has important implications for the politics and future of both sides of the US welfare state:

> The widespread popularity of social tax expenditures may maintain a divided social welfare state that both reduces and increases income inequality by funding progressive public programs as well as regressive tax expenditures. That popularity detracts from the federal government's ability to assuage rising inequality, not just by protecting existing regressive tax subsidies but also by reducing the public demand for more direct and progressive benefits.

Following Howard (Howard, 1997; Howard, 2021; Howard, 2023), Hacker (2002, 2004), and Mettler (2011), Faricy and Ellis (2014, 2021) emphasize the need for social policy scholars to take social tax expenditures seriously, a call consistent with the welfare state financing perspective featured in this Cambridge Element. This is the case because, at least in the United States, looking at how the state might forgo massive tax revenues to promote social policy objectives is a major piece of the welfare state financing puzzle.

Over the last three decades, the literature about the United States dominated the academic conversation on tax expenditures in social policy. This is the case because academic research about social tax expenditures has proved much more limited in scope in most other advanced industrial countries (for early exceptions see Castles 1994 and Greve 1994). For instance, less than a decade ago, Morel, Touzet and Zemmour (2018) wrote that, with a few exceptions (Adema et al., 2011), "in Europe the role of fiscal welfare has remained a blind spot in most social policy studies, national and comparative alike" (550). Yet, they show that, in Europe, tax expenditures and their reforms are important because they play an "instrumental role in the development of private health and retirement insurance plans across welfare states" (Morel, Touzet and Zemmour, 2018: 550). Linked to privatization, the expansion of tax expenditures in various European countries is described as a component of the broader trend towards pro-market social policy restructuring (Morel, Touzet and Zemmour, 2018).

Using a tax–benefit microsimulation model, Silvia Avram (2018) explores the scope and effect on income redistribution of tax expenditures in six European Union countries: the Czech Republic, Denmark, Germany, France, Italy, and Spain. She finds that tax credits and tax allowances "are by no means a policy instrument intended only/mainly for the rich" in these countries, but that "despite being widespread, their distributional consequences are generally not progressive" (284). This leads her to conclude that her research confirms "previous insights from the 'hidden welfare state' literature that suggested tax expenditures are more beneficial to middle and higher income groups" while stressing that "the distributional effects of tax allowances and tax credits are complex and often unanticipated" (284).

In a recent article about Europe, Salvador Barrios et al. (2020b) explore the fiscal and equity effects of social tax expenditure in twenty-eight countries. Focusing on housing, education, and health, they document the widespread use of tax expenditures across Europe (Barrios et al., 2020b: 366). Their quantitative analysis "suggests that the impact of TEs on tax revenues and income inequalities is non-negligible. The redistributive impact of housing TEs is regressive in most countries. Education TEs tend to favour middle- to top-income working-age categories, while health TEs tend to favour the top-income class and the elderly" (Barrios et al., 2020b: 366). These findings are consistent with some of the scholarship on tax expenditures in the United States, which point to their regressive side (Howard, 1997; Mettler, 2011).

In another quantitative analysis, Barrios et al. (Barrios et al., 2020a) explore the fiscal and social effects of tax expenditures for pensions in twenty-eight European countries and find that "the revenue impact of pension-related tax expenditures can be sizeable." More important, and in contrast with some of the US scholarship discussed above, they find that pension-related tax expenditures tend to be progressive by favouring lower-income elderly people and by draining resources from working age individuals at the top of the income distribution through partial or no deduction of pension contributions (Barrios et al., 2020a). These findings are interesting as they point to the diversity of tax expenditures and of their divergent effects on income distribution.

Beyond this type of large-N quantitative comparative analysis and overview publications by international organizations such as the OECD (2010), single country case studies about the role of tax expenditures offer a closer look at the use of this type of fiscal welfare in specific national contexts (Branco and Costa, 2019; Collins and Hughes, 2017; Morel et al., 2019; Provencher et al., 2022; Sinfield, 2020; Stebbing and Spies-Butcher, 2010). Simultaneously, small-N comparative scholarship on tax expenditures is also most helpful. For example, while much of the existing scholarship focuses on liberal welfare states, where the use of tax expenditures has long been extensive, in her recent book *The Politics of Fiscal Welfare*, Nathalie Morel (2025) examines the politics and effects of fiscal welfare in France and Sweden, two contrasted welfare states where the use of fiscal welfare is more recent. Focusing on the example of the introduction of a similar 50 per cent tax deduction on the purchase of domiciliary care and household services, she explores the politics behind the introduction of this tax benefit scheme and its effects on care provision, showing how this scheme has contributed to the privatization of care provision, as well as to inequalities in access to care linked to the highly regressive distributive profile of the benefit. She also highlights the policy feedback effects of this specific policy instrument, which has created powerful vested interests with a stake in defending this tax benefit. Morel's findings for France and Sweden regarding the partisan politics of tax expenditures, the distributive profile of tax benefits, the role of tax expenditures in supporting the privatization of welfare, and the policy feedback effects of this policy instrument are largely consistent with the findings from the United States described above.

For social policy scholars at least, the "hidden welfare state" is no longer hidden, even if the politics of tax expenditures remains understudied in most parts of the globe, with the partial exception of the United States. Yet, even in this country, more research is needed to explore the politics of tax expenditures, including their ideological content and their potential feedback effects of the politics of welfare state reform (Russell, 2018). Tax expenditure literature has primarily focused on its effects on inequality, social divisions, and welfare state politics, particularly regarding welfare state support. However, while tax expenditures by definition involve a loss in state capacity to generate revenues through taxes, their overall impact on states' fiscal capacity has yet to be comprehensively addressed. There are compelling reasons to assume that extensive use of tax expenditures can hinder states' fiscal capacity.

For instance, Mettler's (2018) finding that citizens are less aware of these types of benefits and that this fosters antagonism suggests that the hindering effect of tax expenditures goes beyond the straightforward loss of revenues generated by tax exemptions. One reason is that politics increasingly centres on attaining more tax exemptions instead of creating new or expanding existing programmes that provide cash transfers or public social services.

Furthermore, findings indicate that tax expenditures tend to reproduce and intensify divisions between citizens from different economic classes and particularly benefit high- and medium-income earners. This suggests that when countries go down a less redistributive path, politics will increasingly focus on expanding tax exemptions, further reducing states' revenue capacities in a cycle that can exacerbate itself.

There is a need to integrate different scholarships from public opinion, interest groups, and welfare state politics to examine the political feedback effects from tax expenditures to fiscal development. This interdisciplinary approach could provide a more comprehensive understanding of the long-term implications of tax expenditure policies on state fiscal capacity and social cohesion.

2.3 The Governance and Administration of Financing Instruments

Tax administration refers to how taxes are assessed and collected. From a tax policy perspective, the efficiency of administration is a key concern, as it directly influences revenue collection. Efficiency is typically measured by the ratio between net tax revenue and the potential revenue given tax rates (Kiser and Karceski, 2017). Well-organized systems and modern technologies can significantly enhance revenue outcomes. However, for social policy scholars, tax administration matters not only for efficiency but also because different tax instruments – such as social insurance contributions versus general taxation – are embedded within different governance structures. These structures shape not only revenue collection but also the politics, characteristics, and outcomes of social policy.

The central distinction lies in whether tax administration is centralized or decentralized. In systems where social policy is primarily tax-based and centrally administered, such as income tax and VAT, revenue is pooled into a single fund controlled by the Treasury. This centralization grants the Treasury significant power over social spending, as it controls resource allocation. Fiscal decisions regarding social programmes are integrated into the general budget, allowing the Treasury substantial leverage in determining how much funding welfare programmes receive (Koreh and Shalev, 2017; Truchlewski, 2020).

In contrast, SICs are often governed in a decentralized manner, typically through separate social security agencies (OECD, 2007). In such systems, contributions are managed independently from the general budget, often by semi-autonomous agencies within the state administration or even by social partners, such as trade unions and employer associations, as seen in many European countries (Palier, 2010). This setup reduces the Treasury's control and increases the influence of other actors, such as social partners. This decentralization limits both the capacity and the motivation of the state to intervene in social security funds, thereby shielding social programmes from immediate fiscal pressures (Koreh & Mandelkern, 2023; Manow, 2010).

These structural differences also impact the power dynamics among key actors. In decentralized systems, social partners, such as trade unions, hold significant influence, especially in managing social security funds. For example, French trade unions, despite having relatively low membership density compared to their British counterparts, have been more successful in resisting austerity measures. They have repeatedly managed to compel governments to address fiscal challenges by raising SICs rather than cutting social spending (Truchlewski, 2020).

Moreover, decentralized systems offer greater protection from fiscal pressures (Koreh & Mandelkern, 2023; Koreh & Shalev, 2017). Social insurance funds, managed separately from general budgets, are less vulnerable to budget cuts or political interference, making it harder for governments, especially right-wing parties, to dismantle social rights. In contrast, tax-financed welfare states, where funding is subject to annual budget negotiations and heavily influenced by the Minister of Finance, make it more difficult for left-wing parties to prevent cuts to welfare programmes (Truchlewski, 2020). Hence, when governments impose fiscal consolidation measures to reduce budget deficits, social programmes funded by social insurance are less likely to be cut than programmes funded by general taxes (Jacques, 2024). Instead, governments have political incentives to raise contributions, especially as these increases are often automatic and social partners are able to block cutbacks (Manow, 2010; Truchlewski, 2020).

Recent reform processes in countries with Bismarckian[2] welfare traditions further illustrate the centrality of these administrative structures. These countries – such as Germany, France, Austria, and Belgium – are characterized by social insurance systems primarily funded through employer and employee contributions rather than general taxation and administered by their representatives (social partners), rather than being directly managed by the state. As Palier (2010) explains in *The Long Goodbye to Bismarck*, reforms often targeted the fiscal autonomy of social insurance administrations and sought to centralize control. By increasing social insurance systems' reliance on general tax revenues and shifting decision-making power to the state, reforms gradually eroded the influence of social partners. For example, a 1996 constitutional amendment in France gave parliament the authority to vote annually on the social insurance budget, thereby reducing the system's autonomy. In Germany, the Hartz reforms of the early 2000s diminished the role of social partners in managing unemployment insurance, transferring more control to the state (Hinrichs, 2010; van Berkel, 2010).

These institutional changes in Bismarckian systems were far from merely technical adjustments. By increasing fiscal centralization and enhancing social security agencies' dependence on taxation, these administrative reforms served as prerequisites for later structural changes that cut benefit and altered eligibility criteria (Palier 2010). Similar centralizing processes have emerged beyond Bismarckian systems. In recent decades, tax governance has become increasingly centralized, across various welfare regimes, with reforms unifying the collection and administration of SICs alongside general taxation under the growing control of ministries of finance (Barrand et al., 2004; OECD, 2007). This development suggests that social policy practitioners and scholars should

---

[2] The term "Bismarckian" is derived from Otto von Bismarck, the first Chancellor of Germany, who is credited with introducing the welfare state model in the 1880s. His social insurance programmes, including health, accident, and old age pensions, were among the first examples of state-supported social protection systems, funded through contributions by employers and employees.

pay close attention to administrative-level changes. Understanding these dynamics is crucial, as seemingly technical shifts in governance can have profound implications for social policy outcomes and the protection of social rights.

2.4 Conclusion

Section 2 has explored the complex architecture of welfare state financing, highlighting the diverse array of instruments and structures that modern states employ to fund social programmes. It has shown that welfare state financing systems are far more varied than often assumed, with each instrument and structure having distinct implications for redistribution, programme coverage, and political sustainability. The choice between public and private financing, progressive or regressive tax structures, and centralized or decentralized administration all have far-reaching consequences for social policy outcomes. Moreover, the section underscores that financing is not merely about revenue collection. Rather, it fundamentally shapes the nature of welfare states, influencing everything from programme design to political support.

Given its significant causal impact on social policy, in the next section, we examine the drivers behind the evolution of tax and financing systems, focusing on how fiscal development and welfare state development are intertwined. This exploration will further illuminate the complex relationship between financing mechanisms and the broader landscape of social policy, providing insights into the historical and ongoing processes that shape social policies.

3 How Do Fiscal Development and Welfare State Development Relate?

In the early 1980s, as President Ronald Reagan took office, a new approach to tax policy began to take shape in Washington. Conservative strategists dubbed it "starving the beast," a fiscal strategy aimed at retrenching the welfare state by deliberately reducing government revenues. The plan was straightforward: by cutting taxes and allowing deficits to increase, future administrations would be constrained, unable to expand social programmes, and potentially forced to make cuts (Bartlett, 2007; Klitgaard and Elmelund-Præstekær, 2014; Pierson, 1994).

While the effectiveness of this strategy in curbing US welfare spending remains debatable (Bartlett, 2007; Gale and Orszag, 2004), it highlights a fundamental truth: the emergence and expansion of the modern welfare state is inextricably linked to states' capacity to generate revenue. Without this fiscal capability, large-scale social programmes covering entire populations or significant segments would have been impossible. Moreover, as discussed in the previous section, the particular shapes of states' financing systems (instruments and collection administrations) are causally related not only to revenue capacity but also to states' redistributive capacity and the characteristics of their welfare programmes and allocation logic.

Given the critical importance of fiscal systems in welfare state development, this section explores the drivers behind the evolution of fiscal capacity. It reviews key theories of fiscal development, focusing on how fiscal policies and welfare state expansion are intertwined. We define fiscal development as the process through which countries introduce modern tax instruments, restructure their tax systems, and increase their revenue. As for welfare state development, by contrast, we define it as the expansion, retrenchment, and restructuring of social protection systems, seen in changes to risk coverage, population inclusion, and social spending levels.

This section is organized into three main subsections. The first subsection examines how contingent events and large-scale socio-economic processes have shaped fiscal development, focusing on four key drivers: wars, recessions, modernization, and democratization. The second subsection explores how structural conditions, political struggles, and institutions have influenced the evolution of tax systems and their relationship with welfare states. The final subsection introduces the fiscal contract framework, showing how viewing taxation and social spending as intertwined processes offers new insights into both historical and contemporary social policy dynamics.

3.1 Contingent Events, Socio-economic Processes, and Fiscal Development

The transition from pre-modern financing methods to modern taxation marked a significant shift in fiscal capacity. In pre-modern times, states relied on narrow-based and non-tax revenues, such as plunder, tributes, tariffs, and various specific levies that yielded low tax revenues (Kiser & Karceski, 2017; Morgan & Prasad, 2009). However, starting in the late eighteenth century, the introduction of broad-based modern taxes, such as income taxes, corporate taxes, social insurance contributions, and VATs, marked a significant shift. These taxes, applied broadly and ad valorem, became dominant globally (Genschel & Seelkopf, 2021). This transition, coupled with advancements in tax administration, led to a significant increase in revenues. For example, Scheve and Stasavage (2016) note that tax revenues, which did not exceed 5 per cent of GDP in most countries by 1800, rose to around 9 per cent by 1900 and, in OECD countries, to around 20 per cent by the 1950s.

Social expenditures also increased dramatically as modern welfare states developed in Europe and in North America during the first part of the twentieth century and, especially, after World War II (Myles and Quadagno, 2002). This is the case because welfare states expanded from minimal poor relief to comprehensive systems of social protection covering a wide range of socio-economic risks and needs. This parallel growth in fiscal capacity and social expenditures raises crucial questions about how these two phenomena are related and what explains their concurrent development.

The literature identifies four central drivers of fiscal development that help illuminate both the growth in state fiscal capacity and its key relationship with welfare state development: wars, recessions, modernization processes, and democratization. Some of the accounts suggest that enhanced fiscal capacity enabled welfare state growth, while others indicate that emerging welfare needs drove fiscal development.

Wars stand out as the first major driver of state fiscal capacity. Rooted in theories of state-building, Bellicist theories attribute the growth of fiscal capacity to the enormous financial demands of warfare (Levi, 1989; Spencer, 1897; Tilly, 1992). Wars are costly, requiring states to expand their revenue-raising capacity (Obinger et al., 2018). Furthermore, wars create a favourable environment for tax increases due to the "rally 'round the flag" effect, which reduces public resistance to new and higher taxes (Feldman and Slemrod, 2009; Levi, 1989; Scheve and Stasavage, 2016). In the twentieth century, both World War I and World War II fostered a massive expansion of state taxation power. In the United States, for example, World War II led to a drastic increase in tax rates, transforming the income tax from a "class tax" into a "mass tax" (Scheve and Stasavage, 2016).

Wars also spurred the development of tax administration. During World Wars I and II, innovations like third-party reporting and tax withholding were introduced in the United States, making tax collection more efficient (Kiser and Karceski, 2017; Mehrotra, 2016). For example, during the world wars, the United States introduced two pivotal innovations: third-party reporting and withholding at the source. Third-party reporting required employers to inform tax authorities about workers' incomes, while withholding at the source meant employers deducted taxes directly from pay cheques. These changes marked a significant shift from self-reporting and direct payment by individuals to an employer-mediated system. By enhancing efficiency and compliance, these innovations greatly improved revenue collection.

In Bellicist theories, the direction of causality goes from fiscal development to welfare state development and follows the observation that the enhanced taxation capacity created during wartime tends to persist after the war ends, enabling states to significantly increase welfare spending (Campbell, 1993; Martin et al., 2009; Morgan & Prasad, 2009). This phenomenon termed the "displacement effect" by Peacock and Wiseman (1961) refers to the maintenance of elevated tax levels after the war is over, allowing governments to use the "peace dividend" to finance expanded social and public policies.

Yet, the relationship between fiscal and welfare state development can also work in the opposite direction, when emerging social needs and extended demands for social protection pressure states to develop their fiscal capacity to meet these welfare needs. This is exemplified in the second major driver of fiscal development discussed in the literature: economic downturns (Katzenstein, 1985; Rodrik, 1998; Truchlewski, 2020). Rising unemployment and business losses heighten societal demands for new or extended welfare state programmes, such as unemployment insurance, pressuring states to increase social spending. Simultaneously, economic contraction reduces revenues and access to capital, constraining state finances. As Papadia and Truchlewski (2021) show, this combination of increased welfare demands and reduced revenues compels governments to seek new revenue sources.

Modernization, the third major driver of fiscal development, offers another important explanation for the development of tax systems. Modernization theory has emphasized the roles of industrialization and urbanization for fiscal development, viewing the evolution of tax systems as driven by both emerging social needs and expanding economic opportunities. As societies industrialized, traditional family structures eroded and urban populations grew, giving rise to new social risks such as unemployment and old age poverty (Flora and Heidenheimer, 1981; Montanari, 2001). These changes increased demand for social welfare and greater public expenditure, pushing states to enhance their revenue-generating capabilities (Wilensky, 1974). Concurrently, economic modernization created more taxable wealth, allowing states to implement new and higher taxes without undermining the population's basic needs (Hinrichs, 1966). Modernization processes affect fiscal capacities also by driving state administration capabilities. Wealthier societies are able to better staff and fund their tax administrations, thereby reduce the costs of tax compliance and enhance the efficiency of tax collection (Besley and Persson, 2013).

The fourth major driver of fiscal development identified in the existing scholarship is democratization. The connection between democracy and taxation is rooted in fiscal sociology literature and the fiscal contract approach, which we further describe in Section 3.3. According to this perspective, tax capacity increases when taxation is based on consent rather than just enforcement. This consent is achieved through fiscal contracts where, in exchange for tax revenues, rulers provide their citizens with public goods. Democracy affects tax capacity in two ways: first, democratic institutions lower the transaction costs of creating and enforcing fiscal contracts between taxpayers and rulers (Kiser & Karceski, 2017; Levi, 1989); second, they are argued to cultivate taxpayer consent to paying taxes (Einhorn, 2009).

Interestingly, while fiscal sociology broadly views democracy as enhancing states' fiscal capacities by providing a framework for more effective tax collection, it also sees democracy as a consequence of the state's fiscal imperatives. Tilly (2009), one of the most prominent figures of fiscal sociology, explains that democracy emerged in Europe when states shifted from directly controlling production to relying on taxes from private economic actors for revenue. These actors, in turn, demanded political rights to influence how their taxes were spent, initiating a bargaining process that eventually led to the establishment of representative institutions. Although in the nineteenth century political representation was initially limited to wealthy elites, this process ultimately paved the way for the expansion of the franchise and the attainment of universal suffrage (Tilly, 2009). In fact, relying on oil revenues rather than taxes to fund relatively generous expenditures allows governments of "Petro-states" to stay in power longer, whether they are autocracies or democracies, as they do not have to be accountable to the public regarding the levels of taxes necessary for the public services they receive (Morrison, 2015).

In brief, the relationship between fiscal capacity and welfare state development is complex, with causality flowing in both directions. While welfare needs can drive fiscal evolution, fiscal capacity may also develop independently. Regardless, increased revenue generation expands a government's spending potential and its ability to influence the welfare state. This section has also highlighted the significant impact of contingent events and large-scale economic processes on the adoption of modern taxes and collection systems.

3.2 Structure, Politics, Institutions, Ideas, and Fiscal Development

Equally important are the mechanisms behind these developments, which can be understood through structural conditions, political struggles, institutions, and shifting ideational realms. In Section 3.3, we will critically review how these perspectives offer distinct insights into both the historical formation and current challenges of fiscal and welfare systems, highlighting their limits and the added value of integrating them for a more comprehensive understanding of fiscal development.

Structural explanations focus on the deep, enduring social and economic frameworks within a society that shape the conditions in which individuals and institutions operate. At the economic level, structures refer to how wealth is produced and distributed. At the social level, they encompass systems of social relations, such as class structures or racial and ethnic hierarchies. Demographic structures involve patterns of population growth, age distribution, migration, and urbanization, while geopolitical structures relate to the degree of economic internationalization and global integration.

Central to structural explanations is the idea that these frameworks – or the large-scale trends that change them – are crucial for understanding why societies develop in specific directions. Modernization theory, for example, is a classic structural explanation for the development of modern tax structures and welfare states in the late nineteenth and twentieth centuries. It is considered a structural explanation, because it focuses on how the transition from agriculture to industry, from rural to urban societies, and from feudal to wage-based economies created the foundational conditions for the emergence of modern taxes and the welfare state.

Changing structural conditions are key to understanding recent challenges to states' fiscal and welfare systems. For example, aging populations, a common demographic trend in developed countries, pose significant challenges to welfare state financing by altering the dependency ratio – the number of beneficiaries compared to those funding the system (Kangas and Palme, 2007; Morel and Palme, 2018). Similarly transformative are the effects of economic internationalization, which increases the mobility of people, business, and capital. This enhanced mobility constrains countries' tax policy choices and their capacity to maintain revenue levels while pursuing redistributive goals (Genschel, 2002; Genschel and Schwarz, 2011; Steinmo, 1994).

While structural explanations provide valuable insights into how large-scale changes in society, such as economic shifts or demographic trends, shape fiscal capacity and welfare systems, they can sometimes become overly functional and deterministic. They risk suggesting that specific outcomes are inevitable based solely on these underlying structural trends. This tendency is evident in both early modernization theories and more recent globalization theories (Montanari, 2001; Myles & Quadagno, 2002).

This deterministic tendency was particularly pronounced in early modernization theories, which went beyond seeing industrialization as merely influencing fiscal and welfare development. Instead, it portrayed modern tax structures and expansive welfare states as the inevitable destiny of industrializing societies. According to this view, the transition from agricultural to industrial economies would automatically trigger a universal process of fiscal and welfare expansion, with all modernizing countries eventually converging on similar systems regardless of their distinct historical, cultural, or political contexts (Wilensky, 1974).

Similarly, deterministic in its predictions, though pointing in the opposite direction, globalization theory of the 1990s foresaw an inevitable "race to the bottom." As Genschel (2002) shows, these theories predicted that increasing economic integration and capital mobility would inexorably force states to lower taxes to remain competitive, eroding their fiscal capacity and leading to welfare state retrenchment as governments could no longer sustain social protections (OECD, 1998; Sinn, 1992).

The stark contrast between these structural theories – with modernization predicting welfare state expansion and globalization anticipating welfare state decline – highlights the limitations of purely structural and functional explanations. Rather than converging towards the same outcomes, countries have responded to industrialization and globalization pressures in remarkably diverse ways. For example, in 2022, the average tax revenue and public social spending in OECD countries were estimated to be 34 per cent and 21 per cent of GDP, respectively. Yet, countries like France collected taxes at a ratio of 46 per cent of GDP and spent 31.6 per cent on public social expenditures, while the United States collected only 27.7 per cent of GDP in taxes and allocated 22.1 per cent to public social spending (OECD, 2023, 2024). In fact, while corporate tax rates are certainly influenced by tax competition, other forms of tax revenues, which represent much larger shares of state revenues, are not influenced in the same way (Genschel and Schwarz, 2011).

This significant divergence suggests that structural factors alone are insufficient to explain the evolution of welfare systems and fiscal capacity. Political and institutional factors play a crucial role in shaping fiscal regimes and welfare state development, making them central to understanding why nations follow different paths.

Political and institutional explanations offer a more nuanced understanding of the development of fiscal capacity and welfare state systems than purely structural accounts. Indeed, economic development, in itself, does not lead to a predetermined form of taxation or social protection. Instead, political conflicts, power dynamics, and institutional settings shape a variety of tax regimes and financing models in the modern world (Martin et al., 2009).

Political explanations emphasize the power struggles among labour, capital, and various societal groups, illustrating how their conflicting interests shape tax and social policies. Tax policies are particularly prone to political conflict due to the structure and composition of taxation, which can target distinct economic activities, actors, and classes. For instance, a progressive income tax imposes higher rates on wealthier individuals, facilitating income redistribution. In contrast, a consumption tax, such as a VAT, disproportionately burdens lower-income households, as they allocate a larger share of their income to taxable goods. Additionally, corporate taxes target profits, VAT taxes consumption, and PIT, along with social insurance contributions, tax labour. This complexity can lead to both class-based and sector-based struggles over taxation, reflecting broader redistributive conflicts (Campbell, 1993; Haffert, 2021a).

These diverse political dynamics are apparent in historical examples. In the United States, the push for progressive income taxation was rooted in the broader political currents of the late nineteenth and early twentieth centuries. A broad-based populist movement emerged in response to growing inequality and the concentration of wealth among a few monopolistic capitalists. Populists sought to regulate monopoly capital and address the widening wealth divide, viewing progressive income taxation as a key mechanism to achieve these goals. As Morgan and Prasad (2009) explain, the income tax was incorporated into this broader populist agenda as a tool to discipline capitalists. By shifting the tax burden from consumers paying tariffs to those with high incomes, the income tax became a method for redistributing wealth and addressing the power imbalances between labour and capital.

The introduction of VAT in Europe illustrates redistributive struggles between both sectors and social classes. As Haffert and Schultz (2020) note, the initial struggles over the adoption of VAT in the European Economic Community in the 1960s were largely sectoral rather than class based. Competitive export industries supported VAT as a standardized European consumption tax that would reduce trade barriers, whereas domestic industries opposed it, fearing increased exposure to foreign competition.

These political struggles, however, are embedded within the institutional context in which they take place, and this context shapes both the possibilities and constraints that actors face. Institutions, comprising formal rules, norms, and procedures, play a crucial role in shaping fiscal policies by structuring these political conflicts. They influence the incentives actors respond to and limit the range of policy options available to them. Political regimes, electoral systems, and systems of interest representation all impact the development of tax policies.

For example, democratic institutions, relying on majority rule, were long argued to be central to the development of progressive taxation. This argument was formalized in the well-known median voter model, popularized by Meltzer and Richard (1981), which suggests that democratic institutions empower those who benefit from redistribution. This is because there are generally more individuals on the lower end of the income distribution than on the upper end (i.e., more workers than employers, and more income earners than capital owners) creating an incentive to shift the tax burden onto capital and high-income earners. While the empirical evidence supporting this model for the latter half of the twentieth century is debatable (Iversen & Soskice, 2006; Timmons, 2010), it does align with the situation prevailing during the early twentieth century, when democratization was positively correlated with the adoption of progressive taxes (Genschel and Seelkopf 2021).

In recent decades, however, data suggest that differences in electoral systems – such as majoritarian versus proportional systems – and organized interest representation institutions like corporatism, discussed further in Section 4, play a more decisive role than democracy itself in shaping tax levels and structures (Iversen & Soskice, 2006; Steinmo, 1993). This institutional variation is particularly evident in how different countries responded to global tax competition. While structural accounts predicted that this competition would result in the defunding of mature welfare states, the actual outcomes varied significantly based on the electoral system and its associated institutional constrains (Hays, 2009). For example, under the Conservative majority governments of Margaret Thatcher in Britain (1979–90), the majoritarian system required the approval of just one veto player: the governing party. This allowed Prime Minister Thatcher to implement much deeper cuts compared to Helmut Kohl's Christian-Democratic Union government in Germany, where the proportional system with multiple veto players compelled the chancellor to compromise with coalition partners. This difference in institutional structure illustrates a broader pattern: similar structural pressures, when filtered through varying institutional contexts, can generate different political dynamics and lead to distinct fiscal outcomes (Hallerberg and Basinger, 1998).

One of the central contributions of institutional explanations is the analytical toolbox they offer, particularly concepts like critical junctures and path dependence. These temporal concepts help explain why different countries embark on distinct trajectories in tax and welfare policy. A critical juncture refers to a period of significant change that sets countries on specific paths, which continue to shape their development long after the initial causes have disappeared (Collier and Collier, 1991). Path dependence theory builds on this, emphasizing how institutional choices made at these critical junctures become entrenched over time, leading to the persistence of particular policy frameworks (Pierson, 2000).

The development of tax systems in the United States and France provides compelling examples of how critical junctures can lead to divergent fiscal paths (Morgan & Prasad 2009). Both countries introduced progressive income taxes in the early twentieth century, following heated political debates in the 1890s. However, despite these similarities, their tax systems diverged significantly during and after World War I. In the United States, the income tax became a robust and flexible tool for revenue generation, shaping future fiscal policies and even withstanding conservative attempts to introduce national sales taxes in the 1920s. In contrast, France faced difficulties with income tax collection and consequently shifted towards a national sales tax, which eventually evolved into the VAT. This early divergence in tax policy has had lasting effects, with the United States relying more heavily on progressive taxation and France adopting a mix of regressive and indirect taxes partly to support its welfare state (Morgan & Prasad, 2009).

These historical differences illustrate how institutional paths set during critical junctures continue to shape fiscal and welfare politics today. For instance, the central role of progressive income taxes in the United States has entrenched the country in ongoing political conflicts over revenue generation, while France's VAT has become a significant source of funding for its welfare system. These distinct trajectories highlight the critical role of political institutions and decision-making processes at key moments in determining long-term public finance outcomes.

Political and institutional explanations offer valuable insights into the development of tax systems and welfare states, providing essential tools for understanding why different nations follow distinct fiscal trajectories. While Section 4 of this Cambridge Element explores how these dynamics have evolved into comparative differences in countries' tax structures and trajectories, we must also consider the role of shifting ideas and policy paradigms. This ideational perspective, along with the reciprocal relationship of the fiscal/social contract examined in Section 3.3, provides the necessary foundation for understanding modern welfare financing.

While much of the literature on fiscal development focuses on material interests and institutional constraints, a growing body of research highlights the significance of ideational factors in shaping tax and welfare financing policies. The ideological divide between left and right – where the former generally supports higher and more progressive taxation, while the latter advocates for lower and more neutral taxes – remains a central assumption in studies of taxation. Despite a few exceptions (e.g., Béland and Waddan, 2015; Steinmo, 2003), however, there is relatively little systematic analysis of fiscal developments through an ideational lens, especially as they relate to social policy. Still, existing evidence suggest that shifts in ideas – both about justice and fairness and about the economic consequences of different financing methods – can profoundly affect the trajectory of fiscal and welfare state development.

Policymakers' view on taxation shifted significantly around the time of the Tax Reform Act of 1986, a cornerstone of Reagan-era fiscal policy, which fundamentally altered prevailing notions of what kinds of tax reforms were seen as possible and desirable (Steinmo, 2003). Prior to this, taxation in the

United States was widely seen as both a redistributive and economic policy tool, marked by steeply progressive rates – particularly on "unearned" income, such as capital gains and generous exemptions and deductions intended to steer investments into specific economic sectors. During the 1980s, however, elite views increasingly favoured lower marginal rates, a broader tax base with fewer loopholes, and preferential treatment of capital income (Steinmo, 2003).

Elite perceptions of SICs also shifted significantly in the 1970s (Campbell and Morgan, 2005). Historically, SICs embodied a strong logic of justice and fairness grounded in equivalence and reciprocity (Hinrichs, 1997; Sachweh, 2016). Although public opinion polls consistently showed a stronger support for SICs than for other tax instruments, policymakers from both the left and the right increasingly questioned them – left-wing critics argued that SICs disproportionately burdened low-income earners, while right-wing critics blamed them for driving up welfare expenditures. These shifting perceptions contributed to a significant curtailment of SICs as a primary funding source.

Similarly, perceptions of the economic impact of SICs evolved over time. Throughout much of the twentieth century, SICs were viewed as economically significant not only for their role in social welfare but also for macroeconomic reasons. In the 1940s, Keynesian economists like Harvard's Seymour Harris praised the unfunded character of the new Social Security programme for its ability to stimulate aggregate demand (Harris, 1941). Additionally, as a broad-based tax levied from the first unit of income, SICs were seen as less distortionary than progressive income taxes (Berglass, 1969). These contributions were considered less likely to discourage work and investment compared to the more progressive income taxes. However, by the 1980s, critiques of SICs began to emerge, raising concerns about their economic impact on employment and competitiveness (ILO, 1984; Palier, 2010). In Europe, these shifting perceptions played a key role in reshaping the tax mix of Bismarckian welfare states: while SICs expanded significantly until the 1990s, their relative importance has since declined (Manow, 2010; Palier, 2010).

These examples illustrate how evolving ideas about taxation and financing mechanisms – whether framed in terms of fairness or economic efficiency – can shape fiscal policies in ways that are not reducible to partisan politics or economic pressures alone. An ideational perspective on fiscal development thus offers a valuable complement to existing institutional and interest-based analyses, highlighting how changing perceptions and policy paradigms influence long-term welfare financing trajectories.

The four perspectives – structural, political, institutional, and ideational – discussed in Section 3.2 offer complementary yet distinct insights into fiscal development. Structural explanations provide essential context for understanding the background conditions that shape fiscal policy shifts, such as economic structures, demographic trends, and globalization. However, they often overlook the agency of actors and the role of politics. Political perspectives, in contrast, focus on power dynamics, conflicts, and alliances among different social groups, emphasizing how these struggles shape fiscal policies. Yet, political explanations can be limited by their failure to account for institutional constraints that structure these conflicts. Institutional theories highlight how formal rules, norms, and procedures shape policy outcomes by structuring political conflicts and limiting available choices. These insights are crucial, yet they can overlook dynamic processes that change over time, offering an overly static vision. Finally, ideational explanations emphasize the role of ideas and policy learning in shaping policy possibilities, pointing to how cognitive structures influence policy development. While each perspective contributes valuable insights, integrating them allows for a more nuanced understanding of fiscal policy evolution, illustrating how structural conditions, political power, institutional frameworks, and changing ideas intersect to shape fiscal systems in complex and historically contingent ways.

3.3 The Fiscal/Social Contract

In recent years, social policy scholars have increasingly engaged with the fiscal aspects of welfare states, recognizing their importance in understanding welfare state development, expansion, and current pressures for retrenchment and restructuring (Brownlee, 2003; Pierson, 2001; Steuerle, 1996). This approach has evolved from a more functional perspective, which assumed that the forces driving social spending automatically adjusted financing levels, to a more nuanced view that considers contingency, structure, politics, and institutions as central to explaining countries' fiscal capacities (Haffert, 2021a; Koreh & Béland, 2017).

However, as evident in the preceding review, much of this literature has framed the relationship between fiscal development and welfare state development primarily in terms of revenue availability and its effects on social spending. These accounts can be summarized as follows: when structural, political, and institutional factors, along with contingent events, create resource abundance, they facilitate social spending and welfare state expansion. Conversely, when these factors lead to resource scarcity, they drive expenditure constraints and welfare state restructuring.

Yet, the focus on revenue availability risks oversimplifying social policy by suggesting that other key elements, such as allocation logic or risk coverage, can be studied independently of fiscal policies and politics. This separation, often observed in the academic treatment of fiscal and social policy, overlooks the inherent interconnections between them (Martin et al., 2009; Timmons, 2005).

A more promising approach emerges when social policy is analysed through the lens of the fiscal contract, which frames taxation and social spending as intertwined processes (Koreh & Béland, 2017; Morel & Palme, 2018; Schmitt et al., 2020). This perspective, increasingly embraced in modern tax theories (Kiser & Karceski, 2017; Martin et al., 2009), has gained traction among social policy scholars. It offers new insights into both historical and contemporary social policy dynamics (Béland and Koreh, 2019; Koreh and Béland, 2017). Importantly, it emphasizes that key aspects of social policy, such as the creation of new programmes, allocation logics, redistributive structures and restructuring reforms, can only fully be understood when taxation, and spending politics are considered in tandem (Manow, 2004; Martin and Prasad, 2014; Morel and Palme, 2018; Steinmo, 1993).

The fiscal contract approach views taxation not merely as a revenue extraction process but as a negotiation between states and citizens where tax compliance is exchanged for public goods (Levi, 1989; Schumpeter, 1918/1991; Tilly, 1992). While rulers historically relied on coercion to extract revenue, this method proved costly and risky, leading to conflict, tax evasion, and a loss of legitimacy (Brautigam et al., 2008). Instead, states often engage in a form of quasi-consensual taxation (Levi, 1989) where the provision of collective goods legitimizes their authority and enables increased access to public resources (Brautigam et al., 2008; Levi, 1989; Timmons, 2005).

The concept of taxation as a fiscal contract traces its roots to the founders of fiscal sociology, who portrayed taxation as a tangible social contract – the result of a historic bargain between rulers and the ruled forged in specific times and places (Schumpeter, 1918). These scholars linked the shift from coercion to quasi-consensual taxation to the rise of the tax state. As rulers' personal resources became insufficient to sustain wars, they increasingly depended on taxation, pushing them to forge fiscal contracts with societal elites. Historical instances, such as medieval England's Parliament forcing the monarchy to negotiate with taxpayers, resulted in increased revenues (Kiser and Barzel, 1991). The Glorious Revolution of 1688 also demonstrates this dynamic, as the wealthy agreed to provide the monarchy with revenue in exchange for property and political rights (North and Weingast, 1989).

Fiscal sociology underscores the centrality of the tax state and fiscal contract to the development of the modern state. The need to legitimize revenue extraction prompted states to provide more public goods, leading to the creation of modern institutions, like tax collection bureaucracies and political representation systems, which improved revenue collection and enhanced the credibility of state commitments (Kiser and Karceski, 2017; North, 1993). More recently, scholars have extended this perspective to welfare states, suggesting that social rights and welfare benefits have become integral to the fiscal contract (Morel & Palme, 2018; Schmitt et al., 2020; Timmons, 2005).

However, as Koreh (2017) points out, applying the fiscal contract approach to the study of social policy requires careful adaptation. A review of the literature using this perspective explicitly or implicitly indicates that three adjustments are necessary to fully harness its potential: (1) recognizing the distinct exchange opportunities provided by different financing methods, (2) broadening the notion of the contract to include exchanges between societal groups and the institutional context within they take place, and (3) empirically examining the motivations and dynamics underlying the contract and how it evolves over time.

First, it is essential to distinguish between the various types of exchanges that different financing instruments offer. Earlier studies primarily focused on taxation, often overlooking the significant differences between tax instruments (see, for example, North & Weingast, 1989). Yet, in social policy, whether programmes are financed through general taxation, social insurance contributions, or private financing greatly influences the nature of the exchanges that can take place.

For instance, as discussed in Section 2, SICs that account for an average of 44 per cent of total public social expenditure in OECD countries (Koreh et al., 2024, authors' calculations based on OECD 2022 data) create a direct link between payments and benefits. This system generates specific interests and opportunities for exchange, distinct from general taxation. In social insurance-based systems, the principle of equivalence ("we are entitled because we pay") prevails. It entails a direct relationship between contributions and entitlements, which means that only those who pay into the system, typically through employment, benefit from it. In contrast, general taxation's unrequited nature implies no direct alignment between contributors and beneficiaries. This difference affects the scope of exchange opportunities and has significant implications for welfare coverage and allocation logic.

Moreover, tax and financing instruments also differ in the types of revenue opportunities they create. While tax-based social policies primarily impose spending demands on government budgets, semi- or fully funded social insurance programmes (as well as private funded programmes) can provide governments with access to substantial capital reserves that can address various fiscal and economic needs (Estevez-Abe, 2001; Kangas, 2009; Musgrave and Musgrave, 1973). Koreh and Béland (2017) demonstrate how this characteristic of social insurance played a crucial role in the adoption of key social insurance schemes, as these programmes provided governments with much-needed capital during times of resource scarcity.

Two prime examples of this dynamic are the social insurance programmes introduced by Otto von Bismarck in nineteenth-century Germany and the US federal old age insurance (Social Security) programme established during the presidency of Franklin D. Roosevelt in 1935. While both initiatives were designed to address social needs, such as income maintenance during sickness or old age, their adoption was also driven by fiscal imperatives, as they offered the state access to new revenue streams.

In the German case, Philip Manow (2004) emphasizes that, beyond the widely recognized motivation of Bismarck's social insurance schemes as a countermeasure to the growing labour movement, there was a crucial fiscal and political objective to consolidate the central federal state vis-à-vis the German Länder (provinces) and establish autonomous sources of revenue. At the time, the German federal government had limited taxation authority because the 1871 constitution assigned tax collection powers and veto rights over central government tax increases to the Länder. Bismarck saw the new social insurance programmes as a tool not only to legitimize the creation of new revenue streams but also to remove them from the Länder's control. This allowed the federal state to commit to social protection while gaining a degree of financial independence from the provinces.

Similarly, Leff (1983) identifies a comparable dynamic behind the adoption of the US federal old age insurance (Social Security) system in 1935. In response to the Great Depression, growing federal involvement in the economy during Roosevelt's New Deal led to increased spending and mounting national debt. By implementing old age insurance on a fully funded basis and investing its surpluses in federal bonds, Roosevelt simultaneously addressed public demands for greater economic security and created a reliable, cost-effective source of funding for the federal debt (Jacobs, 2011).

These examples highlight not only the unique exchange opportunities provided by social insurance but also how the state's need for revenue can drive the creation of new social programmes. While this might seem exceptional, recent research suggests that this dynamic is more prevalent than typically recognized in social policy literature. Genschel and Seelkopf's (2021) comprehensive study on the global spread of modern taxes supports this, revealing that during economic downturns, countries are less likely to introduce mass tax instruments, like income tax or VAT, but more likely to adopt SICs. This aligns with the fiscal contract logic that argues, when states urgently need revenue and taxpayers resist regular tax hikes, governments often offer tangible benefits, like social insurance, in exchange for greater revenues.

A second key adjustment to the fiscal contract framework concerns both the actors involved and the institutional context shaping these exchanges. Schumpeter (1918) and Goldscheid (1917/1958), the founders of fiscal sociology, initially conceptualized the fiscal contract as a negotiation between rulers and elites in pre-modern, pre-bureaucratic societies. However, with the expansion of the franchise, the rise of democratic institutions, and the development of complex state bureaucracies, this framework must now account for exchanges, not only between the state and citizens but also among various social groups. Furthermore, both state and welfare state institutions must be seen as shaping and being shaped by the fiscal contract, a dynamic with profound implications for welfare state development.

This expanded view recognizes that modern democratic institutions like electoral systems and mechanisms of interest representation not only allow more actors (e.g., political parties, trade unions, and employers' associations) to participate in the fiscal contract but also enable bargaining and exchanges among them. It also acknowledges that the structure of state institutions shapes these exchanges and affects the range of trade-offs possible.

For example, scholars have pointed out that countries with proportional electoral systems and/or corporatist decision-making frameworks, like Sweden or Germany, are more conducive to consensual policymaking and thus facilitate fiscal bargains between labour and capital. In these systems, labour often concedes to regressive taxation, like payroll and consumption taxes, in exchange for more robust social protections and broader welfare coverage. In contrast, majoritarian systems, such as those in the United States or the United Kingdom, have weaker institutions for consensual policymaking, leading to more intense class conflict. As a result, these countries tend to have more progressive tax systems, but significantly lower social spending (Beramendi & Rueda, 2007; Hertel-Fernandez & Martin, 2018; Steinmo, 1993).

While these scholars did not explicitly use the term "fiscal contract," their focus on how tax and spending politics interact allowed them to explain redistributive patterns across countries that traditional theories struggled with. For instance, key class-based approaches, like the median voter model and power resource theory, suggest that strong labour mobilization should lead to both expanded welfare systems and more progressive taxation (Haffert & Mertens, 2021; Meltzer & Richard, 1981). However, the reality that the largest welfare states rely heavily on regressive payroll and consumption taxes, which disproportionately affect lower-income groups, while countries with smaller welfare states tend to use more progressive taxation, remains puzzling under this framework (Beramendi & Rueda, 2007; Haffert & Mertens, 2021; I. Martin

& Prasad, 2014). We come back to this relationship between tax progressivity and levels of expenditures in Section 4.

The fiscal contract perspective, by accounting for the interplay between taxation and social spending, offers a more nuanced understanding of redistributive outcomes. It also highlights that while general taxation, such as income or corporate tax, may not generate the same exchange opportunities as SICs, it still allows for cross-class and cross-party concessions that shape both tax and welfare policies.

While state institutions, such as electoral systems, shape welfare politics by facilitating certain types of exchanges, welfare politics and policies are also influenced by the welfare state institutions that governments establish to make fiscal and social bargains credible. As Koreh and Mandelkern (2023) explain, the fiscal/social contract has an inherent "time inconsistency problem," where citizens are expected to pay taxes or SICs now, while social benefits, such as unemployment insurance or old age benefits, are realized later. As these authors show, key welfare state institutions like entitlements, indexation mechanisms, and independent social security bodies were originally designed to enhance credibility and trust in state commitments as means to ensure citizens consent to pay into this system. By ensuring the value of future benefits, limiting the discretion of elected officials and delegating decision-making power to social partners and social security bodies, governments signal their long-term commitment to safeguarding citizens' social rights.

The design of these credibility-enhancing institutions mirrors historical fiscal contracts described by North (1993), where time inconsistency also plagued rulers. During wartime, rulers often borrowed money to finance conflicts but had little incentive to repay those loans afterward. This led to demands for political representation as a mechanism to ensure credibility. By granting political representation to those who lent money, rulers could signal their commitment to repay debts and secure future borrowing capacity.

However, like political representation institutions, the influence of social credibility institutions extends beyond merely ensuring trust and payment compliance. Entitlement programmes, for example, create constituencies with a vested interest in maintaining and expanding these programmes. Likewise, delegating decision-making authority to actors, such as social partners and semi-autonomous welfare agencies, generates veto points, creating multiple avenues for these groups to influence and shape social policies over time (Immergut, 1992; Pierson, 2000).

Equally important, these institutions also feed back into tax and financing policies. For example, in an aging society where the population eligible for benefits, like pensions, increases, entitlement-based systems – anchored in legislation with clear eligibility and benefit guidelines – trigger automatic spending increases. This puts pressure on governments to adjust fiscal policies to accommodate rising costs. In contrast, in systems without guaranteed entitlements, where budgets are predetermined, increased demand is generally addressed by reduced assistance levels rather than financing (King, 2000; Koreh et al., 2024; White, 2015).

While institutions, particularly credibility-enhancing institutions, are often associated with self-reinforcing feedback that supports continuity overtime, they can also generate pressures for change through self-undermining effects.[3] As the example of demographic aging suggests, institutional arrangements may compel governments and societal actors to renegotiate existing fiscal contracts. This observation points to a critical yet often overlooked aspect: the need to empirically examine the underlying motivations driving different actors to forge, maintain, or renegotiate these contracts. This brings us to the third key adjustment to the fiscal contract framework.

While classical fiscal sociology often frames the state's primary motivation as revenue maximization and societal interests as focused on either receiving government services or securing political and property rights (Levi, 1989; Schumpeter, 1918; Tilly, 1992), this simplistic attribution of motivations becomes insufficient when considering the variety of financing instruments available and the different types of exchanges they create. Viewing states solely as revenue maximizers highlights the importance of revenue for state survival but fails to explain why some states rely heavily on private funding or pursue policies like tax cuts and the privatization of social benefits. Similarly, assuming that societal interests are limited to what the state provides through spending overlooks broader motivations, such as how social funds are invested and circulated within the economy.

When applying the fiscal contract framework to social policy, it is therefore crucial to consider not only public but also private modes of finance and to empirically examine, rather than pre-attribute, the motivations of the parties involved. In fact, various scholars have shown that state involvement in establishing and regulating pension systems in the twentieth century was closely tied to state-building objectives (Béland & Koreh, 2019; Kangas, 2009). Importantly, while some countries achieved these objectives through public financing, others relied on private financing methods, illustrating that states can pursue their goals through various funding approaches beyond tax revenue maximization.

---

[3] On the distinction between self-reinforcing and self-undermining policy feedback, see Jacobs & Weaver, 2015.

Canada's province of Quebec and Japan exemplify these contrasting approaches to achieving similar state-building objectives. In the mid-1960s, Quebec's state- and nation-building efforts led it to establish a separate contributory public pension plan (the Quebec Pension Plan) alongside the programme covering people in the rest of Canada (the federal Canada Pension Plan) allowing the province, through a newly established public investment board (*Caisse de dépôt et placement du Québec*), to invest pension fund surpluses to drive provincial economic development (Béland and Koreh, 2017). In contrast, post–World War II Japan implemented a private pension system that was crucial for state-building by accumulating large reserves of patient capital. These highly regulated funds were directed towards public infrastructure and industrial development, helping Japan rise to global prominence (Estevez-Abe, 2001; Park, 2011). These cases also suggest that business consent to co-finance workers' pensions rested not only on labour relations but also on their potential benefits from investing these funds.

Recognizing that both states and key societal actors can have vested interests in private financing modes is particularly important to understand the evolution of the fiscal and social contract, especially in recent decades. From a revenue maximization perspective, the wave of pension reforms across OECD countries in the 1990s might seem puzzling, as these reforms generally involved reductions in public benefits alongside the expansion of private, pre-funded pension schemes (Ebbinghaus, 2011; Hassel et al., 2019; Orenstein, 2013). However, as a growing body of literature on financialization suggests, when states perceive financial markets as critical growth drivers or as sources for financing public debt, they may have vested interests in pension privatization as a way to create and strengthen financial markets (Fastenrath et al., 2017; Maman, 2021; Trampusch, 2018). Furthermore, the growth of finance has empowered financial actors like insurance companies, whose interests in private pension provision have been argued to be a major driver of pension privatization reforms (Kemmerling and Neugart, 2009; Naczyk and Palier, 2014), altering the fiscal contract by increasingly tying pensions to financial markets and their performance.

3.4 Conclusion

To summarize, this section has explored the complex relationship between the development of fiscal systems and welfare states to examine the deep connections between taxation and social spending. Through an analysis of contingent events, socio-economic processes, structural conditions, and political-institutional factors, the section has demonstrated how the evolution of tax systems has both enabled and been shaped by welfare state development. It has also highlighted how different financing methods, from general taxation to SICs and private funding, create distinct exchange opportunities and shape social policy outcomes in various ways.

This section explains why the fiscal contract framework is a valuable analytical tool for social policy scholars. By focusing on the mutually causal relationships between taxation, finance, and welfare programmes, this perspective offers more comprehensive accounts of welfare state development and restructuring than traditional approaches. For scholars of social policy, the fiscal contract framework enhances our ability to understand multiple dimensions of welfare state politics. The framework helps explain the adoption timing of different programmes, illuminates why certain coverage and redistributive features are chosen over others, and provides insights into processes of both continuity and change in welfare states. By taking the tax and finance side seriously, this analytical approach broadens our understanding of welfare policies and politics, offering more intersecting explanations for empirical puzzles that have challenged conventional theoretical frameworks. As the section has shown, viewing taxation and social spending as fundamentally intertwined processes, with welfare benefits integral to the modern fiscal contract between states and citizens, provides a more nuanced and complete picture of how welfare states develop, adapt, and transform over time.

4 Fiscal Foundations of Welfare State Diversity

From the 1970s onwards, scholars began to observe a notable fact: while welfare states had expanded considerably across advanced economies, they had also begun to diverge. This divergence was most visibly reflected in differences in levels of social expenditure – one of the earliest and most concrete indicators of variation. These differences sparked the development of a robust field of comparative social policy focused on mapping welfare state diversity, tracing its sources, and evaluating its consequences (Myles and Quadagno, 2002). One of the most influential contributions is Gøsta Esping-Andersen's Three Worlds of Welfare Capitalism (1990), which proposed a typology of welfare state regimes: Liberal (Anglo-American), Conservative (Continental), and Social Democratic (Nordic). His work showed that welfare states differ not only in how much they spend but also in their institutional logics, design features, and redistributive outcomes.

What is less emphasized, however, is that Esping-Andersen (1990) also highlighted differences in how welfare state regimes are financed. This insight has inspired a growing body of research on the fiscal side of the welfare state –

classifying countries based on the level, composition, and structure of their tax systems. While these tax regime clusters do not always map neatly onto Esping-Andersen's typology, they offer crucial insights. Scholars have shown that tax systems help explain persistent differences in welfare state generosity, institutional form, and redistributive outcomes (Campbell and Morgan 2005; Ganghof 2006; Kato 2003; Kemmerling & Truchlewski 2021; Martin 2015; Prasad and Deng 2009; Steuerle 1992; Wilensky 2002).

This section builds on that literature to examine the comparative significance and origins of tax regimes in shaping welfare state diversity. We use the term 'tax regime' here as a shorthand for the specific configuration of fiscal traits within a country, focusing on comparative differences rather than proposing a rigid typology. The first part reviews how cross-national differences in tax levels and structures help explain variation in three core dimensions: (1) the level of welfare spending, (2) the institutional design of social protection, and (3) redistributive outcomes. To make sense of these divergences between tax regimes, the second part draws on three major explanatory perspectives from the comparative political economy literature – the functionalist, the distributional, and the sectoral (Haffert, 2021a) – to account for how these tax regimes emerged and became institutionally embedded.

4.1 The Comparative Impact of Tax Systems on Welfare State Variation

Generous welfare states tend to exhibit significantly higher tax levels. Countries within Esping-Andersen's Conservative–Continental and Social Democratic–Nordic clusters – what Jonas Pontusson (2005) calls "Social Europe" – have average tax-to-GDP ratios around 42.2 per cent, compared to 28.6 per cent in the Anglo-American (Liberal) cluster.[4] These differences in fiscal effort are reflected in public social expenditure levels: 26.5 per cent of GDP in Social Europe versus 18.9 per cent in Liberal America.

This variation seems to support a standard assumption: governments tax more because they choose to spend more. However, research increasingly challenges this view. It suggests that tax structures do not just mirror spending decisions – they also shape them. The instruments used to raise revenue significantly affect a state's capacity to support expansive welfare systems.

Empirical comparisons support this. The European cluster relies more heavily on consumption taxes (e.g., VAT) and SICs. Consumption taxes account for 12.1 per cent of GDP in Europe, compared to 8.2 per cent in the Anglo-American cluster. Social insurance contributions are even more

---

[4] In Section 4.1, we use data from the OECD Tax Database from 2019.

divergent: 12.6 per cent in Europe (13.9 per cent excluding Denmark[5]) compared to just 3.9 per cent in the Anglo-American group. They are even higher in countries that rely on Social Health Insurance systems (Austria, Belgium, France, and Germany), in which health expenditures are largely funded by social insurance contributions. Income taxes, by contrast, are similar across clusters as a share of GDP, but in Liberal regimes, they constitute a larger share of total taxation, indicating a narrower and more progressive base.

These differences matter. As discussed in Section 2, tax instruments vary in their revenue-generating capacity for both economic and political reasons. Economically, consumption taxes are less distortionary and more growth compatible than income taxes (Lindert, 2004). Politically, taxes differ in visibility and in their link to perceived benefits. Social insurance contributions, for example, are typically deducted automatically from wages and are matched by employers' contributions, making them relatively invisible. More importantly, they are closely tied to social entitlements. As a result, many people perceive SICs not as taxes but as contributions to their own pension or health insurance plans (Campbell & Morgan, 2005; Morel & Palme, 2018; Schmitt et al., 2020).

4.1.1 Tax Composition and the Character of Welfare States

The composition of taxation does more than shape revenue – it influences the institutional character of welfare states. This is particularly true when countries rely on tax instruments that establish a direct link between contributions and benefits. In conservative welfare regimes, particularly in Continental Europe, SICs form the backbone of welfare finance. As Manow (2010) argues, SICs define the structure of Bismarckian welfare systems: eligibility depends on contribution records, benefits are earnings related, financing is payroll based, and governance typically involves corporatist representation by employers and employees.

In contrast, liberal regimes like the United States use the tax code to subsidize private welfare provisions. Rather than expanding public programmes, they offer tax breaks that disproportionately benefit middle- and upper-income earners, fostering a privatized and unequal welfare state (Hacker, 2002). In 2019, US tax expenditures for social purposes equalled 3.5 per cent of GDP, far above levels in most European countries. As Morel and Palme (2018) note, the liberal tax regime is unique in the extent to which it channels social spending through the tax system (tax breaks for social purposes represent on average 1.8 per cent of GDP in Anglo-American democracies).

---

[5] With almost no social insurance funding (0.3 per cent of GDP), Denmark is an outlier within the European cluster regarding reliance on social insurance contributions. Instead, it relies heavily on personal income taxes, reaching 24.5 per cent of GDP, which is more than half its total tax take.

Both liberal and social democratic regimes rely on general taxation, but for very different ends. Social democracies use general taxes to fund universal, citizenship-based benefits, while liberal regimes support residual, means-tested systems targeted at the poor. Because general taxation is unrequited and does not establish a direct link between payments and benefits, it offers greater institutional flexibility. Unlike SICs or tax expenditures, which tend to embed specific entitlement logics and governance structures, general taxation does not inherently constrain the design of social protection. As a result, although liberal and social democratic regimes draw on similar revenue tools, the logic of allocation differs fundamentally.

4.1.2 Taxation and Redistribution

Redistributive outcomes also vary significantly among countries. According to the OECD (2018), Anglo-American countries reduce inequality through taxes and transfers by only 20–25 per cent, compared to 30–40 per cent in most Social European states. These differences reflect not just variations in policy instruments but also deeper institutional and political configurations.

As discussed in Section 2, Korpi and Palme (1998) famously argued, there is a "redistribution paradox" on the transfer side: systems that provide universal or earnings-related benefits – thereby incorporating middle- and high-income earners into the welfare system – are more successful at reducing poverty and inequality than systems that rely heavily on means-tested programmes targeting the poor (Brady and Bostic 2015; Jacques and Noël 2018; Korpi and Palme 1998). However, this paradox is not limited to the transfer side. As Prasad and Deng (2009) show, a similar dynamic exists on the taxation side. Nordic and Continental welfare states, which achieve high levels of redistribution, rely more heavily on regressive tax instruments, such as VAT and SICs than their Anglo-American counterparts. These taxes broaden the base and ensure stable, high levels of revenue, even though they are less progressive in structure. In fact, a government cannot fund a generous welfare state without having either high VAT or high SICs, which is an important lesson for progressive reforms in Anglo-American democracies.

In contrast, Anglo-American welfare states often emphasize more progressive income and property taxes. Indeed, the Anglo-American cluster relies slightly more on property taxes (2.8 per cent of GDP relative to 1.9 per cent in the European cluster), especially in Canada and the United Kingdom (4 per cent of GDP each). However, because these are concentrated on a narrow group of high earners and often paired with extensive tax expenditures, they raise less revenue and support more modest welfare commitments. In practice, as Morel and Palme (2018) and Hacker (2002) have shown, the apparent progressivity of Anglo-Saxon tax systems is frequently offset by the regressive effects of tax breaks for private social spending, such as deductions for employer-sponsored health and pension plans, which disproportionately benefit higher-income groups while reducing public revenue capacity.

Building on this insight, Guillaud et al. (2020) highlight a further trade-off: countries that emphasize greater tax progressivity often do so at the expense of overall tax capacity. In other words, as with benefits, there is a tension between progressivity and size – a flatter, broader tax system may be less progressive in formal terms but more redistributive in practice because it supports more expansive public provision. Taken together, these findings suggest that effective redistribution is not achieved through vertical progressivity alone. Rather, it depends on a combination of revenue-generating capacity and of the inclusive design of social programmes, which together sustain the political coalitions necessary for redistribution at scale.

Taken together, these studies call for a critical revision of conventional understandings of welfare state finance. Revenue levels are not merely the outcome of spending decisions – they are shaped by the design of tax systems. Differences in tax instruments and the structure of taxation play a significant role in shaping welfare state diversity, particularly in explaining variation in fiscal effort, the character of social protection, and redistributive outcomes. By analysing how states fund their welfare systems – not just how they spend – fiscal perspectives offer essential insights into the institutional and distributive architecture of social policy across countries.

4.2 Three Perspectives to Explain Tax Regimes

Having established the significance of taxation for shaping the structure and outcomes of welfare states, the next section turns to a deeper question: What explains the emergence and persistence of such different financing systems across countries? A conventional view holds that the development of tax policies mirrored the construction of the welfare state and was shaped by the same political and institutional forces. A traditional version of classical power resource theory, for instance, posits that left parties develop more generous welfare states funded by high and progressive taxes (Cameron, 1978). However, this theory struggles to explain a critical empirical puzzle: countries dominated by left parties often achieve higher levels of social spending, yet paradoxically rely more on regressive forms of taxation than countries in which the left never governs (Martin, 2015; Andersson, 2022). To make sense of this divergence between tax regimes, the following section draws on three major explanatory perspectives from the comparative political economy literature: the functionalist, the distributional, and the sectoral perspectives (Haffert, 2021a).

The functionalist perspective offers a structural explanation for differences in countries' tax systems, emphasizing that tax structures emerge as a response to two main imperatives: countries' spending needs and the constrains imposed by the economic environment. In functional accounts, governments first decide on spending levels and then select tax instruments that are economically viable given broader structural conditions (Ganghof, 2006; Lindert, 2004). A core assumption is that in order to sustain high levels of social expenditure, governments are functionally compelled to adopt tax instruments that minimize economic distortions and maximize revenue. In a situation of international tax competition, capital mobility and a structural dependence of the state on capital (Przeworski and Wallerstein, 1988), governments face a critical challenge: how to generate sufficient revenue without discouraging job creation or capital investment. This constraint leads them to prefer taxes that generate substantial revenue with minimal economic distortion. Hence, according to the functionalist account, the reliance of high-spending welfare states on regressive taxation such as VAT stems from its status as one of the most efficient revenue-generating machines, especially when compared to capital and corporate taxes, which generate relatively little revenues, while potentially creating significant economic distortions (Lindert, 2004).

The functionalist perspective also links tax regime variation to structural economic conditions: countries with open economies – more exposed to capital flight and global competition – are seen as more compelled to adopt business friendly taxes like VAT, creating a distinctive relationship between economic openness and tax structure (Seelkopf et al., 2016).

While the functionalist perspective offers important insights into the structural constraints shaping tax regimes, it faces two key critiques. First, institutionalist accounts challenge its assumption of present-day optimization by emphasizing the long-term effects of early policy choices. These accounts argue that tax structures are not simply functional responses to current spending needs or economic pressures but are instead shaped by path-dependent processes. Kato's (2003) analysis of tax regimes reflects this view. In contrast to functionalist accounts that see the adoption of VAT as a response to the need to generate higher revenues, Kato reverses the causal relationship. Drawing on a path-dependent institutional logic, she shows that countries that adopted VAT early on were in better position to fund social policy expansions at a later point in time. In contrast, late adopters did not have the necessary revenue base when international tax competition intensified in the 1980s and constrained their ability to rely on other forms of taxes (Kato, 2003).

A second critique comes from the distributive perspective, which challenges the functionalist tendency to downplay political agency by treating structural pressures as uniform constraints. Instead, distributive accounts emphasize that both spending and taxation are shaped by political conflict and institutional variation across welfare state regimes.

An influential distributional perspective has emerged through the notion of tax bargain, which helps explain why European countries tend to reach a high tax and high spending equilibrium, whereas Anglo-American democracies do not (Andersson, 2022; Beramendi and Rueda, 2007; Jacques, 2020; Martin, 2015; Steinmo, 1993; Timmons, 2010). This approach conceives taxation as a negotiated bargain between political actors, shaped by their competing objectives around expenditure and revenue extraction. It highlights how similar structural pressures, when mediated by different institutional contexts, can produce divergent fiscal trajectories.

Two key institutions take centre stage in this perspective: the electoral system and the system of interest group representation. Both proportional electoral systems and a specific system of interest group representation called a "coordinated market economy" (CME) (Hall and Soskice, 2001) help foster a high tax, high spending bargain between employers, unions, and political parties across the ideological spectrum. In contrast, institutional complementarities between majoritarian electoral systems and non-corporatist, liberal market economies (LMEs) tend to generate lower overall tax revenues, more modest welfare states, and generally more progressive tax structures. This divergence reflects not only the incentives created by electoral rules but also how the broader organization of the economy influences the feasibility and direction of tax and spending bargains.

Electoral systems influence three factors that are crucial for tax policy choices: political stability, parties' responsiveness to the median voter, and political incentives regarding public spending. Majoritarian electoral systems are characterized by single-party governments that concentrate power and generate barriers to entry for smaller parties. Moreover, they are characterized by adversarial policymaking and policy volatility, because a minor change in votes can lead to a large difference of seats won. In contrast, proportional representation (PR) systems are characterized by multiparty systems, more consensual forms of policymaking in coalition governments, and greater political stability, as small shifts in the electorate generally do not alter the balance of power and opposition parties are still able to maintain an influence on policymaking (Lijphart, 2012).

The stability in PR systems creates the conditions for reaching bargains between political actors in which the left achieves its egalitarian objectives with generous social spending rather than via progressive taxation, whereas the right ensures that capital holders do not disproportionally pay for higher spending. Furthermore, the risk associated with losing power is smaller, as opposition parties maintain an influence on policymaking because of coalition or minority governments and influential parliamentary committees (Andersson, 2022). Hence, left governments can pursue a strategy of funding expansions of social spending drawing on regressive taxes, even if the revenues they generate are not allocated exclusively to social programmes, as is the case of SICs. Knowing that they can block future right-wing governments that could be tempted to cut back social spending, left governments can credibly commit to tax the middle class and the poor with VATs and use this revenue source to fund more generous social spending (Andersson, 2022; Steinmo, 1993; Timmons, 2010). Hence, PR systems are associated with an earlier adoption of VAT (Helgason, 2017).

In majoritarian systems in contrast, it is impossible for parties to credibly commit to a long-term tax and spending strategy. If a party is thrown out of office in a system of single-party government, it cannot maintain its influence on the next government. Hence, the left refrains from implementing regressive taxes to fund generous social spending because a future right-wing government could choose to reduce social spending to fund income tax cuts while maintaining regressive taxes. Because of the absence of credible commitment between parties in majoritarian systems, right-wing parties cut taxes, while left-wing parties increase taxes on the rich, but refuse to increase taxes on their own supporters (Andersson, 2022).

Electoral systems also influence how political parties respond to the preferences of the median voter. Research indicates that voters generally support two interconnected tax-related objectives: higher tax progressivity targeting the rich, and lower overall taxation rates, especially reduced consumption taxes that affect all citizens (Barnes, 2015; Barnes et al., 2024). Majoritarian and PR systems differ markedly in how they translate these voter preferences into political strategy. Two-party systems are more likely to converge towards the centre, because small shifts in votes have large effects in majoritarian systems, whereas parties are more insulated from having to rapidly react to voters' changing moods in PR systems (Finnegan, 2022). Hence, parties in majoritarian systems are more likely to adopt a short-term tax strategy pleasing as many voters as possible, preferably by using tax expenditures beneficial in districts that are key to their re-election, therefore limiting their efforts to broaden the tax base.

Electoral systems are also related to political incentives regarding tax and spending levels. Proportional representation systems are more likely to result in coalition governments. Because the multiple players involved in the budget process can block cutbacks that would displease their constituencies, it is more difficult to reduce spending in coalition governments (Hallerberg and Von Hagen, 1997). Moreover, left-wing parties, which are associated with more spending and taxes than parties on the right, tend to have more electoral success in proportional systems, while right-wing parties are stronger in majoritarian systems (Döring and Manow, 2017). Hence, revenues and expenditures tend to be higher in countries with PR systems than in countries with majoritarian systems (Iversen and Soskice, 2006).

There are institutional complementarities between electoral systems and systems of interest group representation, as coordinated market economies have PR systems and liberal market economies have majoritarian systems (Beramendi et al., 2015). Within each of these two models, both the political and economic institutions create mutually reinforcing incentives regarding taxation. These typologies of systems of interest group representation are derived from the Varieties of Capitalism school that focuses on the preferences of employers to understand why they consent to large welfare states in some countries but not in others (Hall and Soskice, 2001). These institutions also contribute to reaching or failing to achieve the high (regressive) tax and high spending bargain. While theories based on the role of electoral systems focused on parties, those relying on Varieties of Capitalism focus on producer groups like unions, but especially employers.

Coordinated market economies are characterized by macro-corporatist institutions, where peak association representing unions and employers meet with government representatives to implement public policies related to wages, taxes, and spending. Another key distinguishing feature of CMEs is their unique industrial structure, which differs fundamentally from liberal market economies. These economies depend on workers with industry-specific skills that are not easily portable. This specialization creates a significant vulnerability for workers, who risk losing everything if their specific industry declines. To offset this 'skill risk' and encourage long-term specialization, employers consent to expansive social insurance systems. This provides the necessary security for workers to invest in specialized skills, forming the foundation of the high-tax, high-spending corporatist bargain (Hall and Soskice, 2001).

This industrial structure and the accompanying institutional arrangements fundamentally shape the tax and welfare regime strategies. The engagement of unions, employers, and the state in macro-corporatist institutions makes it possible to credibly commit to tax policies. Repeated contacts between unions and employers can raise awareness of both constituencies on the costs of high capital taxes on firms' competitiveness and on the benefits of social insurance spending for employees' retention (Martin, 2015). In CMEs, employers and unions can consent to a tax and spending policy bargain that involves high social spending paid for by taxes on workers. Employers consent to high social insurance since they can tailor tax policies to their own needs, notably by making sure that the tax burden is not disproportionately theirs to shoulder. Unions consent to higher taxes on their own members, knowing that they can count on higher social spending (Jacques, 2020; Martin, 2015).

In contrast, in LMEs, industries rely on general skills, reducing the employer's motivations to support public social insurance. Employers and unions are not represented by a peak association, rather they represent the particular interest of their own industry and hence cannot impose bargains on their members. Unions and employers aim for short-term objectives and prefer to shift the tax burden to the other group. The conflictual relationship between employers and unions makes the high tax/high social insurance bargain impossible to sustain in LMEs (Jacques, 2020; Martin, 2015).

The corporatist/non-corporatist character of these capitalism varieties fundamentally shapes tax regime differences. In CMEs, the corporatist structure constrains the left's ability to rely on capital taxes to fund social spending as such actions would disrupt corporatist agreements between labour and capital. Hence, we also observe that CMEs are associated with an earlier adoption of VATs (Helgason, 2017). In contrast, non-corporatist settings allow the left more flexibility with capital taxation. At the same time, in non-corporatist settings, left-wing parties may hesitate to increase regressive taxes, fearing these won't genuinely fund expanded social spending. Consequently, they might prefer higher income taxes on the wealthy.

These distributional accounts are based on stylized assumptions about political parties and interest groups preferences that are not necessarily tested by these theories. They assume that actors know the consequences of tax policies, make tax policy choices based on known distributional effects, and that each actor aim to maximize their own welfare, defined either in terms of income (for producer groups) or of votes (for parties). However, the relationship between parties' tax policy preferences and those of voters is inherently more complex than what these rationalistic theories suggest, as we will discuss in Section 5. Moreover, the sectoral perspective reveals that producer groups may also have more nuanced preferences.

While distributional accounts emphasize class-based conflicts and compromises between labour and capital in tax regime formation, the more recent sectoral perspective shifts towards a cross-class view of tax policy choices, rooted in growth model theories (Haffert, 2021a; Haffert, 2021b; Haffert and

Mertens, 2021; Huo, 2021). The growth model perspective builds on the Varieties of Capitalism school to explain how countries engage in different strategies to achieve durable economic growth (Baccaro and Pontusson, 2016; Baccaro et al., 2022). It distinguishes between export-oriented growth models and consumption-oriented growth models, which resemble CMEs and LMEs, respectively, although some countries combine both growth models (i.e., Sweden) and others are unable to develop a coherent growth model (i.e., Italy). Growth models are sustained by cross-class social blocs uniting labour and capital in the economic sectors that benefit from the current growth model (Baccaro and Pontusson, 2016; Baccaro et al., 2022).

The sectoral perspective on tax policy choices proposes that taxes can be used as industrial policies to encourage specific sectors and economic activities as they influence decisions related to savings, consumption, working, exporting, importing, and investing (Haffert 2021b; Steinmo 1993). Haffert and Schultz (2020) note that the conflicts surrounding the introduction of VAT in 1967 in the European Economic Community were primarily reflecting sectoral rather than class-based interests. Because VAT is generally regarded as a regressive tax method that disproportionately impacts low- and middle-income classes, researchers often assume that the struggles over its implementation are class based. While this is accurate in terms of VAT's expansion, Haffert and Schultz (2020) reveal that the initial political struggles over its adoption in the European Economic Community were sector based. Competitive export sectors advocated for its introduction, needing a standardized European consumption tax to reduce trade barriers, while domestic industries resisted the change because it exposed them to foreign competition.

According to this perspective, the size and structure of the tax state depend on the balance of power between different sectoral coalitions that are influencing tax policy. For instance, both unions and firms in sectors that depend on domestic consumption will favour lower consumption taxes (Haffert, 2021a). In contrast, Nordic countries rely heavily on service sector jobs and tax consumption so that citizens find it more attractive to rely on public services (Haffert, 2021a). Moreover, countries that rely on financial assets to finance debt-driven consumption will maintain a more favourable treatment on mortgage interest to encourage debt-financed home ownership (Fuller, 2015) and foster higher property value. In turn, higher property value can generate larger property taxes as a proportion of GDP, as seen in Section 4.1.2 in the case of Canada and the United Kingdom. Therefore, countries with consumption-driven and domestically oriented growth models maintain less consumption taxes and aim to tax production with direct taxes, whereas countries with export-driven growth models minimize taxes on producer groups and shift the tax burden towards consumption to curb it and to encourage exports (Haffert and Mertens, 2021).

Still, apart from the pioneering work of Lukas Haffert, research on the link between growth models and tax regimes remain in its infancy and more needs be done to develop the sectoral perspective in order to explore the relationship between growth models and tax policy choices. More generally, future research should integrate the three perspectives together to explain the determinants of tax regimes. In fact, they are generally presented as separate theories by researchers, but the sectoral and distributional perspective are relying on similar variables and institutions to explain tax regimes (consumption-oriented growth models tend to have majoritarian electoral systems and a Liberal market economy for example), whereas both perspectives certainly agree that structural constraints highlighted by the functional perspective matter to explain tax policy choices.

The three perspectives share rationalist assumptions that political actors know the distributional effects of tax policies and choose them based on their own interests and on the institutional constraints that they face. Yet, future research could incorporate a constructivist perspective focusing on how political parties and producer groups perceive tax policies and their distributional effects, and whether these policies are deemed politically feasible or not (see, for example, Fastenrath et al., 2022).

4.3 Conclusion

The analysis of tax regimes reveals a complex interplay between economic structures, political institutions, and social compromises. While different theoretical perspectives – functionalist, distributional, and sectoral – offer unique insights, they collectively underscore that tax systems are not simply technical instruments but deeply political mechanisms reflecting societal negotiations and economic strategies.

Across different welfare state models, we observe a paradoxical pattern where seemingly progressive objectives are achieved through ostensibly regressive taxation mechanisms. The European cluster demonstrates how high social spending can be funded through consumption taxes and SICs, challenging simplistic notions of tax progressivity and highlighting the nuanced relationship between taxation, redistribution, and economic growth.

Future research should focus on integrating these perspectives and developing a more comprehensive understanding of welfare financing. This includes examining both public tax systems and private financing instruments to provide a more holistic picture of the comparative dimensions of the welfare finance

5 Public Opinion on Taxation

equation, moving beyond their current compartmentalization to explore how different funding mechanisms interact and shape social policy and socio-economic outcomes.

Taxation is the lifeblood of social policy, providing the resources needed to fund social protection systems, deliver quality welfare services, and mitigate economic inequality. However, the sustainability of these systems depends not only on technical design but also on public consent. Fiscal sociology emphasizes that while taxation is legally mandated, its legitimacy rests on societal perceptions of fairness, trust in government, and alignment with broader social values.

While the previous section examined macro-level theories on how institutions and structural pressures shape tax policy decisions, this section shifts focus to the micro-level, exploring how public opinion influences the politics of taxation. Understanding public attitudes towards taxation is essential for social policy scholars because public preferences shape the feasibility of tax reforms, the redistributive potential of tax systems, and the broader political dynamics of welfare state governance. Governments' ability to expand the welfare state is not solely constrained by economic limitations but also by citizens' willingness to support higher taxation (Karceski and Kiser, 2020). In other words, taxation is as much a political challenge as it is an economic one, making public opinion a critical factor in understanding welfare state development.

Contrary to assumptions that tax preferences simply reflect socio-economic status or ideological leanings, research shows that attitudes towards taxation often follow counterintuitive patterns (Goubin et al., 2026; Jacques, 2023). As Section 5.1 demonstrates, individuals' preferences for taxation are shaped by a range of factors beyond self-interest, including perceptions of fairness, institutional trust, and historical policy legacies. Mapping these preferences provides insight into the political feasibility of tax reforms, particularly efforts to raise revenue for expanding social programmes.

Following this Element's emphasis on policy feedback theories, Section 5.2 examines how past tax policy choices shape contemporary public opinion. Specifically, we analyse how the main revenue-generating instruments discussed in Section 2.1 influence public perceptions and how major historical drivers of fiscal development – such as wars and economic recessions, discussed in Section 3.1 – continue to shape attitudes towards taxation. This discussion highlights gaps in current research on how tax policy decisions create feedback loops in public opinion and identifies directions for future study. Section 5.3 then explores tensions between elite and public preferences on taxation and asks whether public opinion genuinely influences tax policy choices.

This section does not aim to provide a comprehensive literature review on public opinion and taxation. Rather, it focuses on two core dimensions that are crucial for social policy: attitudes towards tax progressivity and attitudes towards tax levels and willingness to pay. Tax progressivity is a key mechanism for redistributing income from the wealthy to the broader population, while overall tax levels determine the extent to which a welfare state can sustain generous social programmes. By examining public attitudes towards these issues, this section sheds light on how individual beliefs, contextual factors, and political processes interact to sustain or challenge the fiscal foundations of the welfare state.

5.1 Determinants of Tax Policy Preferences at the Individual Level

The study of public opinion on taxation has witnessed significant developments in recent years. From relatively vague survey questions about general support for taxation, the field has evolved towards using more complex online tools to survey the intricacies of the public's preferences regarding taxation. These include direct trade-off questions comparing support for public spending with and without the costs associated to it (Busemeyer et al., 2018), conjoint experiments measuring how specific tax policy changes influence opinion (Bremer and Bürgisser, 2025), and online budget tools that allow respondents to simulate a public budget by choosing how to fund their preferred public programmes (Barnes et al., 2022; Tuxhorn et al., 2021). The literature has highlighted three main individual-level determinants of preferences for taxation: self-interest related to one's socio-economic status (income and education), ideology, and fairness considerations.

Self Interest

Many models of public preferences on taxation (and on the welfare state in general) rely on rationalist assumptions based on individuals' self-interest. Higher-income citizens are more likely to be net contributors to the welfare state since income reduces the need for social protection and increases the amount of tax paid in proportional and progressive tax systems (Meltzer and Richard, 1981). Hence, some studies have found that higher income is correlated with support for lower levels of taxation (Sumino, 2016).

Self-interested motivations are also reflected in a widespread tendency to prefer other income groups to foot the bill of the public spending that people demand. Respondents prefer lower tax rates on their own income bracket (Ballard-Rosa et al., 2017). Moreover, renters are more in favour of property taxes than homeowners (Bowler and Donovan, 1995), non-smokers prefer more cigarette taxes than smokers (Green and Gerken, 1989), and the poor prefer income taxes to sales taxes (Donovan and Bowler, 2022). In fact, most citizens prefer to shift the tax burden towards high-income citizens, as few people consider themselves to be rich and most individuals believe that they themselves belong in middle income groups (Fernández-Albertos and Kuo, 2018; Cansunar, 2021). Hence, support for progressive taxes on the rich is very high (Barnes et al., 2024; Barnes, 2015; Cansunar, 2021; Mathisen, 2024), while people do not necessarily support higher levels of taxation because it would involve that they have to pay higher taxes themselves (Barnes, 2015; Sumino, 2016).

Rationalist models based on self-interested assume that citizens resist higher taxes, because the costs of taxes are directly visible to them more so than the public services funded by taxes (Downs, 1960). However, while pundits and politicians tend to assume that governments are punished by the electorate if they increase taxes (Fastenrath et al., 2022), there are relatively few cross-national studies on the electoral consequences of tax policy changes (Ahrens and Bandau 2024; Foucault et al., 2017; Tillman et al. 2009;). Most studies on this issue focus on a single country and are inspired by retrospective voting models, in which voters' preferences are essentially a reaction to governments' past policy decisions. They find that governments' popularity (Geys and Vermeir, 2008a; Geys and Vermeir, 2008b) and vote share (Ahrens and Bandau, 2024; Johnson et al., 2005) tend to decline when they increase taxes, but that broad-based taxes policy changes have more (negative) electoral impact than tax increases concentrated on few rich voters (Tillman and Park, 2009).

However, consistent with some form of negativity bias, tax increases may be punished, but tax cuts are either unrewarded (Finseraas, 2012) or only very weakly rewarded (Ahrens and Bandau 2024). Studies also suggest that right-wing governments are more likely to be rewarded for tax cuts than their left-wing counterparts (Ahrens and Bandau, 2024; Tillman and Park, 2009).

Moreover, support for tax cuts decreases significantly when respondents are faced with the costs of lower taxes, for instance in the form of cutbacks to public services (Bremer and Burgisser, 2025). Therefore, politicians opposed to tax cuts can highlight the fiscal trade-offs they entail to reduce public support for them. Still, more remains to be done to study the electoral consequence of tax reforms, especially considering there are very few international datasets adequately measuring tax policy reforms. Additionally, the dependent variables used in these studies (vote shares in elections, government popularity, or vote intentions) can be influenced by several other factors than just tax policy changes that remain difficult to model properly.

Yet, the literature on tax policy preference has largely departed from rationalist assumptions and has shown that the relationship between individual income and tax preferences is not as straightforward as commonly assumed. First, people misperceive their position in the income distribution (Cansunar, 2021) and are largely misinformed about the consequences of tax policies (Bartels, 2005). Hence, they are more likely to follow their perceived self-interest than their material self-interest. As such, informing people about their position in the income distribution influences their preferences for tax progressivity. The poor are much more likely to demand higher taxes on the rich when they become informed that they are technically poor (Fernandez Albertos and Kuo, 2018).

Second, having a sufficient level of income is a necessary condition for willingness to pay taxes. Individuals living in precarious financial situations may feel that an additional tax burden is unfair or would significantly decrease their well-being. Although low-income people may want more public expenditures, they prefer to shift the tax burden to higher-income individuals. Studies on the phenomenon of wanting "something for nothing," that is, demanding higher public spending but lower taxes, find that economic vulnerability correlates with support for lower taxes and support for more spending (Edlund and Johansson Sevä, 2013; Goubin et al., 2026). Hence, some studies have found a positive relationship between income and willingness to pay taxes, at least among certain groups (Tuxhorn et al., 2021; Jacques, 2023).

Education's relationship with tax policy preferences departs from self-interested perspectives. Indeed, while more educated people are more likely to be net contributors to the state and to have more financial security, education correlates positively with support for higher tax levels and with willingness to pay (Barnes et al., 2024; Jacques, 2023). This is because education is related to several factors that increase willingness to pay such as information, patience, trust, and fairness beliefs (Jacques, 2023). More educated citizens have a better understanding of the necessity to pay taxes to sustain public services and have a better knowledge of the tax system, whereas misperceptions about its functioning lead to lower satisfaction with it (Eriksen and Fallan, 1996). Research has shown that political information moderates the effect of income on support for tax progressivity. High-income individuals do not display lower support for progressive taxes if they are politically informed, possibly because these respondents understand that relatively high taxes can lead to positive social outcomes that they value more than a marginal improvement to their own material well-being (Stiers et al., 2021).

Moreover, higher education is associated with patience. Patient citizens are more likely to accept paying higher taxes today to improve the public services they will likely receive in the future (Wang, 2017). Education also correlates with higher social and institutional trust (Hooghe et al., 2012), relates to more willingness to pay taxes (Barnes, 2015; Habibov et al., 2018; Lachapelle et al., 2021; Tuxhorn et al., 2021), and with willingness to sustain the costs of policy reforms (Garritzmann et al., 2023). Furthermore, citizens with less education are more likely to hold negative views of unemployed individuals receiving social assistance or unemployment benefits, as they want to maintain a distinction between themselves and those further down the social hierarchy (Van Oorschot, 2006). In contrast, more educated citizens do not need to stigmatize the unemployed to maintain their social status (Attewell, 2022). Taxpayers are more willing to pay to fund state spending allocated to citizens whom they deem deserving (Stanley and Hartman, 2018). In brief, while rationalist perspectives dominated the study of voters' reactions to tax reforms, individual-level determinants of tax preference depart from pure self-interested motivations. Indeed, higher income and more educated respondents are not necessarily against higher taxes, while the poor and less educated are not staunch supporters of tax increases.

Ideology and Fairness

In contrast to the nuanced association of income with tax policy preferences, there are very clear ideological divides in the public's opinion on taxation. Left-wing individuals tend to believe that taxes are lower, less progressive, and less detrimental to the economy than the right does (Stantcheva, 2021). Left-wing respondents are more likely to prioritize public services rather than cutting taxes, whereas the right prefers lower taxes, even when the cost of tax cuts in terms of higher debt or cuts to public services are made salient (Bremer and Bürgisser, 2025). The left puts more value on the public services that taxes are paying for and is ideologically committed to income redistribution. While the left draws on ability-to-pay principles and highlights the importance of taxes in sustaining public services, the right tends to reject higher taxes and is less likely to support tax progressivity and higher taxes (Barnes, 2015; Donovan and Bowler, 2022; Mathisen, 2024). In the United States, for instance, Republicans are much less likely than Democrats to support higher taxes on the rich, but they share generally progressive tax policy preferences, as both the right and the left prefer lower taxes on the poor than on other income groups (Ballard-Rosa et al., 2017). In fact, tax increases on the poor tend to violate fairness norms and to be punished by voters of all parties (Ahrens and Bandau, 2024).

Several studies have also analysed how ideology filters the impact of self-interest on support for taxation (Armingeon and Weisstanner, 2022; Jacques, 2023). They have been interested in analysing how cross-pressured individuals (e.g., a high-income leftist or a low-income rightist) resolve the tension between their self-interest and their ideology that are pushing their preferences in different directions. Left-wing individuals resolve this tension by prioritizing their ideology over their self-interest (Armingeon and Weisstanner, 2022; Bremer and Bürgisser, 2025; Jacques, 2023). In fact, ideology influences the weight that being a net contributor to the state has on citizens' preferences (Armingeon and Weisstanner 2021).

Ideology also influences perceptions of the fairness of taxation. For instance, right-wing individuals are more likely to believe in meritocracy and trickle-down economics, which influences their attitudes towards taxation (Hope et al., 2023). Indeed, perceiving that income is derived from hard work or luck influences attitudes towards taxes, because people are less likely to support higher taxes on the rich if they believe that income is due to hard work (Alesina and La Ferrara, 2005; Ballard-Rosa et al., 2017; Cavaillé 2023). Informing survey respondents that a large proportion of the wealth of the top 1 per cent comes from inheritance (and therefore luck) significantly reduces support for tax cuts for the rich (Hope et al., 2023). When the distribution of income is perceived as unfair and benefiting the rich, citizens are more likely to demand higher taxes on the rich to compensate for this unfairness and to change the unequal distribution of market incomes (Cavaillé, 2023; Scheve and Stasavage, 2016).

The Coalitional Politics of Tax Reforms

The findings of the research on determinants of preferences for taxation have several consequences for the politics of tax reforms. While the public maintains an overall preference for more progressive taxes, we do not observe an overwhelming support for raising or even just maintaining tax levels to sustain the desired level of public services. The most generous welfare states, however, have traditionally been funded by broad-based taxes paid for by a very large proportion of the population, rather than by concentrating tax increases on relatively few affluent citizens (see Section 4). Tax competition, the relatively high elasticity of capital income to taxation, and the small number of high-income citizens put some limits to the potential size of tax revenues to be extracted from a higher taxation of the rich (Lindert, 2004). Hence, parties that want to expand the size of the pie to fund additional social policies have to perform a delicate balancing act to gather a pro-tax coalition.

The issue of taxation may facilitate or hinder coalition building between different groups and parties. Our own research has argued that taxes represent an additional wedge within the coalition that left-wing parties aim to form between sociocultural professionals and low-skilled service and production workers (Jacques, 2023). Sociocultural professionals, such as university-educated workers in interpersonal occupations, often in the public sector, are the group most willing to pay taxes (see also Bremer and Bürgisser, 2025). Indeed, they have high education and tend to be ideologically oriented towards the left, two factors that are strongly related to support for higher taxes. As such, they figure at the core of a coalition to expand the welfare state's redistributive capacity and ensure its fiscal sustainability. In contrast, service and production workers, another constituency that traditionally is voting for the left, are significantly less willing to pay as they are poorer and less educated. Jacques (2023) finds that among the right, income and education reduce support for higher tax levels, whereas on the left, individuals with more income and more education are more willing to pay taxes than those with lower income and education. Similarly, high-income leftists are more likely to support progressive fiscal policies than low-income leftists (Bremer and Bürgisser, 2025).

The unwillingness to pay of a large proportion of their constituents puts centre-left parties in a difficult situation. On the one hand, they need to raise taxes if they want to increase spending. On the other hand, they must otherwise implement cutbacks in some policy areas to fund additional spending in other policy domains which may contribute to tensions between their core electoral constituencies. Raising taxes may alienate their support among lower incomes and less educated groups. Yet, the willingness to pay of sociocultural professionals offers a silver lining for centre-left parties. If progressive parties can propose a unifying policy agenda bridging tensions among groups, sociocultural professionals may represent key voters willing to contribute to a more generous welfare state (Jacques, 2023). Taxing the rich, but also the upper middle class, comprised of sociocultural professionals, might be an avenue to consider for social-democratic parties to fund an ambitious social policy agenda.

5.2 How Tax Instruments and External Events Feedback into Preferences

Section 5.1 has analysed the determinants of individual preferences on taxation and their consequences for the politics of tax reforms. In this subsection, we turn the tables and analyse how tax policies feedback into public opinion since tax policy design influences how the public feels about various taxes (Campbell, 2018). We discuss how three main dimensions of revenue-generating instruments discussed in Section 2, influence public opinion: the progressivity of taxes and of social policies, the degree of public and private funding, and the governance structure of the funding mechanism. Then, we analyse how external events like wars and economic downturns influence tax policy preferences.

An important strand of this literature has analysed whether the size, progressivity, and degree of redistribution of the spending and taxing dimensions of the welfare state influence public opinion. On the one hand, the reciprocity argument suggests that citizens are more willing to pay taxes if they expect to receive something in exchange for the taxes they pay (Levi, 1988). Therefore, if social policies are universal, in the sense that the whole population is allowed to receive benefits or services, citizens are more likely to be willing to pay taxes and, as a consequence, the social budget should be larger and therefore more redistributive (Jacques and Noël, 2018; Korpi and Palme, 1998).

In line with this argument, Berens and Gelepithis (2019) have found that support for tax progressivity is higher when the middle class benefits from the welfare state, and lower when social spending is targeted at the poor. Similarly, tax progressivity, but more importantly social transfers' progressivity, increases the effect of income on preferences for redistribution (Beramendi and Rehm, 2016). Hence, less progressive social transfers would dampen class conflict about taxation. This argument is contested, however, as another study has found that both more redistribution and more progressivity in social transfers generates bigger class cleavages concerning support for redistribution (Fernández and Jaime-Castillo, 2018). In fact, the relationship between social policy universalism and willingness to pay suggested by Korpi and Palme (1998) deserves more direct empirical tests.

Section 2 highlighted the importance of the funding mechanism and the governance structure of taxation. We can assume that SICs are perceived differently by the public than income taxes. Some argue that SICs are perceived as deferred wages rather than taxes (Palier, 2010), and that it is very easy for the public to see where the money goes, which would increase their popularity (Campbell, 2018). The fact that SICs are tied to the programmes they are funding could help to build credible policies and enhance citizens' trust (Koreh and Mandelkern, 2023). In fact, some have found that support for social insurance programmes like Social Security in the United States is very high because the payment is directly earmarked to a popular social programme whose beneficiaries are deemed deserving of the benefits they received because they contributed to the programme (Campbell, 2018; Williamson, 2017). However, more research needs to be done to analyse how citizens perceive social security contributions relative to other forms of taxation. Are citizens more willing to pay social contributions than taxes? One study has shown that SICs are the least contested type of tax across twenty democracies (Martin and Gabay, 2018), but another study has found that in the United Kingdom, SICs are not particularly popular (Barnes et al., 2024). Moreover, we do not know if the nature of the programme funded by SICs influences public opinion: Are respondents more supportive of paying pension contributions that are more likely to be seen as deferred wages than healthcare contributions common in Social Health Insurance systems? Are contributions to social insurance covering life cycle risks (pensions and healthcare) inherently more popular than contributions for social insurance coverage of a more targeted labour market risk like unemployment insurance? Hence, more research should be done to confirm if funding by SICs is politically easier to sustain.

Similarly, public opinion on private financing methods is also understudied. As discussed in Section 2.1, private funding of social policies entails significantly less redistribution than funding by income taxes or social security contributions. It is expected that the beneficiaries of private financing methods would oppose an expansion of public financing that would crowd out private insurance. Moreover, several studies have found that private financing shapes public opinion as it reduces support for the state's involvement and influences expectations about the provision of social services by the market (Busemeyer and Iversen, 2020; Lindh, 2015; Zhu and Lipsmeyer, 2015). Hence, private financing methods would create a vicious circle against the public funding of social policies by increasing support for the private system among its beneficiary and potentially reducing citizens' willingness to pay taxes for the public system.

However, most of the previous research on the influence of privatization of funding on public opinion rely on time series cross-sectional designs that cannot establish causality, mostly because of the lack of long panel series of public opinion that include the relevant questions on support for specific public or private programmes. Future research must identify a semi-exogenous programmatic change in financing methods towards private or public financing and rely on a panel survey of public opinion to see if the programme changes influence the public in the expected direction.

External Events

Individuals' tax preferences are not only influenced by tax policy design but also by large-scale external events. For example, as discussed in Section 3, during World Wars I and II, income tax rates on the rich increased significantly to fund the war effort. To explain this phenomenon, Scheve and Stasavage (2016) argue that these quasi-confiscatory top marginal tax rates seen in Anglo-American democracies were driven by a public narrative about the necessity to compensate the population for their sacrifices during the war. While average citizens were conscribed to participate in mass war mobilization, rich citizens could avoid conscription, and many industries profited from the war economy. Hence, the conscription of men made it fairer to demand the conscription of wealth. As such, high progressive taxes were seen as a measure to re-establish the equal treatment of all citizens (Scheve and Stasavage, 2016). Similar arguments are put forward during financial crises, especially if they are accompanied by a public bailout of the financial sector, as citizens want to be compensated for bearing the brunt of the economic crisis. Thus, support for progressive taxes and for tax rates on the rich tend to increase during economic crises (Garcia-Muniesa, 2019; Limberg, 2020).

However, economic crises may have distinct effect on preferences regarding the level of taxation. As individuals become worse off, they might become less willing to provide resources to finance policies that partly benefit themselves and partly benefit others. Because individuals seek to preserve their incomes and their consumption, when their income decline, they prefer to reduce the taxes they pay to maintain their disposable income and current consumption level. Hence, when economic growth is high, citizens' real incomes are rising and governments can increase taxes without reducing citizens' consumption level (Streeck, 2014).

Taxes can therefore be seen as a luxury good for which demand decreases when income declines. Morals and ideology are also a luxury good. As voters become richer, their moral values, or ideology, become more important to them, whereas self-interest matters more when they become poorer (Enke et al., 2022). In fact, exposure to economic recession generates greater "selfishness" and less willingness to contribute to the common pool in laboratory studies (Fisman et al., 2015). Moreover, cross-national, panel, and longitudinal analyses reveal that subjective and objective income decline is associated with lower support for tax levels (Jacques and Weisstanner, 2022; Vlandas et al., 2024).

These findings suggest that the impact of income growth have important consequences for welfare state politics. In advanced industrial societies, during the post–World War II era of welfare state expansion, growing incomes made it politically easier for governments to increase levels of taxes to fund social policy expansion, as they could raise taxes without reducing citizens' take-home pay. Since then, social expenditures have continued to increase due to population aging, lower economic growth, the maturation of welfare state commitments, and the transition to a post-industrial service economy (Pierson, 1998). Yet, governments have not increased taxes to pay for these expenditures. Rather, tax revenues have been stagnant on average in advanced democracies since the end of the 1980s (Karceski and Kiser, 2020), whereas public debt has exploded (Streeck, 2014). This may be explained by the fact that the last four decades in advanced democracies have been characterized by an absence of wage growth for a large proportion of the population, which has led to a decline of the "taxability" of post-industrial societies, as it becomes difficult for governments to impose higher taxes on citizens (Jacques and Weisstanner, 2022; Streeck, 2014).

5.3 Are Governments Reactive to Public Opinion on Taxation?

Political parties are reactive to public opinion, at least under certain conditions (Busemeyer et al., 2020). However, the previous review suggests that policy elites may have different preferences than the general public. For example, there seems to be strong public support for funding social policy by SICs, but policy elites are often wary of SICs' effects on employment, as it increases labour costs and reduces firms' competitiveness (Kemmerling, 2009). Moreover, experts on climate change praise the merits of carbon taxes but sustaining high enough levels of carbon pricing to influence consumers and producers' decisions is often politically difficult to achieve because of the public's resistance (Carattini et al., 2018). While policy elites may prefer broad tax bases that are economically efficient and hard to avoid, such as VATs, citizens often prefer narrow tax bases on rich citizens and corporations (Steinmo, 2003; Barnes et al., 2024).

The policies resulting from the disagreements between the public and policy elites on taxation is a fascinating research topic. This is illustrated in the following debate over government's responsiveness to taxes on the rich. Sometimes, tax policies do not follow public preferences. This is the case regarding taxes on the rich. As shown in this section, there is an overwhelming support for higher taxes on the rich. In fact, increasing taxes on the rich would even increase overall support for tax reforms (Bremer and Bürgisser, 2025). At the same time, the national income share allocated to the top 1 per cent has risen in most countries over the last decades and there are significant revenue needs across OECD countries. However, governments have generally refrained from increasing taxes on the rich, such as by raising top marginal tax rates, taxes on capital gains, inheritance taxes, or wealth taxes. Can this phenomenon be explained because governments are more responsive to the preferences of the rich, or is it because support for taxes on the rich is not as pervasive as generally assumed?

Since the publication of Gilens and Page (2014) classical study on the issue, it has become common to argue that the policy process in most democracies is biased in favour of the preferences of high-income citizens and of the interest groups representing them, while being unresponsive to those of median voters. Some argue that the lack of reforms towards increasing the tax burden on the rich represents a case of unequal responsiveness, because tax cuts on the rich are opposed by a majority of voters (Mathisen, 2024). Hence, parties would not be responding to the public's demand for higher taxes on the rich.

However, rather than blaming unequal responsiveness, some contend that the public's preferences on taxes on the rich are elusive. Indeed, some taxes that target mostly the rich, such as inheritance taxes, are very unpopular (Emmenegger and Marx, 2019). Moreover, even if they support higher taxes on the rich, citizens tend to be indifferent to how much higher taxes on the rich should be raised, which gives leeway to governments that do not wish to implement significant reforms (Ballard-Rosa et al., 2017). Also, many people concerned about inequality do not believe that progressive taxes are the main solution to the problem as they hold strong beliefs about the importance of the equal treatment of individuals by the state, which means, to them, that everyone should pay the same rate of taxes (Scheve and Stasavage, 2023).

Finally, there is a large difference between what people say in surveys and the extent to which they demand taxes on the rich in the real world. In focus groups, people display strong internalized pro-business tax preferences and meritocratic justifications of wealth. As such, politicians often perceive survey responses about taxes on the rich to be meaningless to actual politics and believe that there is no appetite among voters for taxing the rich (Fastenrath and Marx, 2023). For policies to change, the party system must supply electoral pledges about taxes on the rich (Elsasser et al., 2023). Yet, left-wing parties have generally converged with the right regarding wealth-related taxes in the 1990s (Lierse, 2022). Moreover, the logic of collective action suggests that tax reform targeting a few rich voters or corporations are likely to be resisted by the groups concerned, whereas few interest groups form to defend citizens' interest to improve the revenues sources of the general budget to have better funded public services. This debate suggests that there is room for development of more qualitative tools of public opinion research that can provide different insights into the political dynamics of taxation.

5.4 Conclusion

In summary, this section has critically reviewed studies on the microfoundations of tax policies by focusing on public opinion dynamics. It revealed that preferences for taxation and for public spending are not driven by the same factors, as income, income growth, and education have somewhat counterintuitive associations with tax preferences. We have also reviewed studies revealing strong contextual effects on tax preferences as citizens react to the existing tax and spending system differently when forming their preferences. Finally, we have argued that more studies need to be done on public opinion of specific taxes and on causal impact of tax changes on government's popularity, as assumptions about the unpopularity of tax increases may not be as straightforward as commonly expected.

6 Conclusion

As US Supreme Court Justice Oliver Wendell Holmes Jr. (1841–1935) famously stated in a key court case: "Taxes are what we pay for civilized society" (quoted in San Juan, 2018: 45). Today the term "civilized" might sound outdated and problematic but, in concluding this Cambridge Element on taxation and social policy, it is appropriate to modify that quote and simply stress that taxes are the price we pay for the welfare state.

In fact, as discussed in this Cambridge Element, taxation is at the foundation of the modern state and, historically, fiscal development and welfare state development are closely intertwined. This is why social policy scholars should take a close look at specific fiscal policy instruments, including SICs (Béland & Koreh, 2017) and tax expenditures (Howard, 1997) that are strongly embedded in modern welfare states. Simultaneously, as suggested in this Cambridge Element, scholars have much to gain from engaging with the broader fiscal literature on tax regimes and on preference formation. These remarks are important because, as we suggested in Section 1, for too long, welfare state researchers have focused far more on the spending side of social policy than on its revenue side, despite the fact that the former cannot exist without the latter (Béland & Koreh, 2017; Campbell, 1993; Martin et al., 2009; Morgan & Prasad, 2009).

The publication of this Cambridge Element and the existence of some of the excellent fiscal scholarship on social policy reviewed in the above sections point to the fact that this unfortunate situation is being corrected, one book or paper at a time. This is the case with regard to the comparative study of welfare state development, the analysis of concrete tax instruments, the critical assessment of the increasing reliance on private social policy funding, the discussion about tax regimes as they interact with social programming, and, finally, public opinion about taxation, which is becoming increasingly rich and sophisticated. Among these issues, the growth in private funding stressed in this Cambridge Element requires particular attention, especially because it has long been identified as a key aspect of contemporary welfare state restructuring (Gilbert, 2002). More generally, even social policy scholars who focus on the benefit side of things ignore these rich fiscal literatures that shed crucial light on the tax infrastructure of welfare states and the concrete policy instruments that structure the relationship between taxation and social policy.

While our Cambridge Element sets the agenda for future research on welfare state financing and the fiscal side of social policy through a critical review of existing literature streams, we acknowledge its exclusive focus on the Global North is a key limitation. Nevertheless, we hope that scholars working on the Global South will still find our discussion of Global North literatures useful.

Importantly, some issues that are central to tax and social policy debates in the Global South are much less central in contemporary debates about taxation and social policy in the Global North. One notable example is the case of informal workers who constitute the vast majority of the labour force in many developing countries, a situation that requires to take a new look at the concept of social contract in this specific economic, social, and taxation environment (Rogan, 2022).

Conversely, theories of fiscal development, developed with the Global North in mind, might still offer valuable lessons about the challenges of creating comprehensive and fiscally sustainable social policy systems in the Global South – particularly in regions like sub-Saharan Africa, where tax collection remains so difficult due partly to a large informal sector and tax evasion at the top (e.g., Moore, Prichard and Fjeldstad, 2018). More scholarship is needed to establish whether the patterns that have been found in the Global North can help explain fiscal and social policy development elsewhere.

This broader intellectual project will require greater attention to factors that are less central in most Global North contexts, such as the enduring legacies of colonialism (Frankema and Booth, 2020) and the role of international organizations such as the World Bank (Okunogbe and Santoro, 2023), which are typically most relevant for understanding politics and public policy in the Global South.

While scholars studying the Global South might benefit from engaging with the literature about the Global North, the opposite is also true. Examining countries in different regions of the world could help scholars based in the Global North to gain a richer comparative understanding of the diverse ways in which taxation and social policy interact across time and space.

Partly because of the work of international organizations like the International Labour Organization and thanks to global social policy scholars like Bob Deacon (2007), North–South exchanges in social policy research are increasingly common. This trend should foster more comparative fiscal scholarship that bridges the North–South divide while expanding knowledge on fiscal development, fiscal social policy instruments, private funding, tax regimes, and public opinion about taxation.

References

Adema W, Fron P, and Ladaique M (2011) Is the European welfare state really more expensive?: indicators on social spending, 1980–2012; and a manual to the OECD social expenditure database (SOCX).

Ahrens L and Bandau F (2024) The electoral consequences of taxation in OECD countries. *Electoral Studies* 88: 102774.

Alesina A and La Ferrara E (2005) Preferences for redistribution in the land of opportunities. *Journal of Public Economics* 89(5–6): 897–931.

Andersson PF (2022) Taxation and left-wing redistribution: The politics of consumption tax in Britain and Sweden. *Comparative Politics* 54(2): 279–301.

Armingeon K and Weisstanner D (2022) Objective conditions count, political beliefs decide: The conditional effects of self-interest and ideology on redistribution preferences. *Political Studies* 70(4): 887–900.

Aspalter C (2018) Real-typical and ideal-typical methods in comparative social policy. In Greve B (ed.) *Routledge handbook of the welfare state*. Routledge, pp. 314–328.

Attewell D (2021) Redistribution attitudes and vote choice across the educational divide. *European Journal of Political Research* 61(4): 1080–1101.

Avram S (2018) Who benefits from the "hidden welfare state"? The distributional effects of personal income tax expenditure in six countries. *Journal of European Social Policy* 28(3): 271–293.

Baccaro L, Blyth M, and Pontusson J (2022) *Diminishing returns: The new politics of growth and stagnation*. Oxford University Press.

Baccaro L and Pontusson J (2016) Rethinking comparative political economy: the growth model perspective. *Politics & Society* 44(2): 175–207.

Ballard-Rosa C, Martin L, and Scheve K (2017) The structure of American income tax policy preferences. *The Journal of Politics* 79(1): 1–16.

Barnes L (2015) The size and shape of government: Preferences over redistributive tax policy. *Socio-Economic Review* 13(1): 55–78.

Barnes L, Blumenau J, and Lauderdale BE (2022) Measuring attitudes toward public spending using a multivariate tax summary experiment. *American Journal of Political Science* 66(1): 205–221.

Barnes L, de Romément J, and Lauderdale BE (2024) Public preferences over changes to the composition of government tax revenue. *British Journal of Political Science*. 54(4): 1457–1467.

References

Barr N (2002) Reforming pensions: Myths, truths, and policy choices. *International Social Security Review*, 55(2): 3–36.

Barrand P, Ross SG, and Harrison G (2004) Integrating a unified revenue administration for tax and social contribution collections: experiences of central and eastern European countries. Washington, DC: International Monetary Fund (WP/04/237). www.imf.org/en/Publications/WP/Issues/2016/12/31/Integrating-a-Unified-Revenue-Administration-for-Tax-and-Social-Contribution-Collections-17834.

Barrios S, Coda Moscarola F, Figari F, et al. (2020a) Size and distributional pattern of pension-related tax expenditures in European countries. *International Tax and Public Finance* 27: 1287–1320.

Barrios S, Figari F, Gandullia L, et al. (2020b) The fiscal and equity impact of tax expenditures in the European Union. *Journal of European Social Policy* 30(3): 355–369.

Bartels LM (2005) Homer gets a tax cut: Inequality and public policy in the American mind. *Perspectives on Politics* 3(1): 15–31.

Bartlett B (2007) "Starve the beast": Origins and development of a budgetary metaphor. *The Independent Review* 12(1): 5–26.

Béland, D and Waddan, A (2015) Breaking down ideas and institutions: The politics of tax policy in the USA and the UK. *Policy Studies*, 36(2): 176–195.

Béland D and Koreh M (2017) The fiscal side of social policy: State building, payroll contributions, and pension reform in 1960s Canada. *Journal of Policy History* 29(4): 594–613.

Béland D and Koreh M (2019) Social insurance as fiscal policy and state-building tool: the development and politics of payroll contributions in Israel and Canada. *Journal of Social Policy* 48(1): 1–20.

Bellafiore R (2018) Tax Expenditures Before and After the Tax Cuts and Jobs Act. *Tax Foundation, Washington, DC*, https://taxfoundation.org/tax-expenditures-pre-post-tcja.

Beramendi P, Dincecco M, and Rogers M (2019) Intra-elite competition and long-run fiscal development. *The Journal of Politics* 81(1): 49–65.

Beramendi P, Häusermann S, Kitschelt H, et al. (2015) *The politics of advanced capitalism*. Cambridge University Press.

Beramendi P and Rehm P (2016) Who gives, who gains? Progressivity and preferences. *Comparative Political Studies* 49(4): 529–563.

Beramendi P and Rueda D (2007) Social democracy constrained: Indirect taxation in industrialized democracies. *British Journal of Political Science* 37(4): 619–641.

Berens S and Gelepithis M (2019) Welfare state structure, inequality, and public attitudes towards progressive taxation. *Socio-Economic Review* 17(4): 823–850.

Berglas E (1969) Financing the defense budget. *Rivon Lekalkala*, (62): 144–150.

Besley TJ and Persson T (2013) *Taxation and development*. In Auerbach AJ, Chetty R, Feldstein M, and Saez E (eds.) *Handbook of public economics*. Elsevier, pp. 51–110.

Bowler S and Donovan T (1995) Popular responsiveness to taxation. *Political Research Quarterly* 48(1): 79–99.

Brady D and Bostic A (2015) Paradoxes of social policy: Welfare transfers, relative poverty, and redistribution preferences. *American Sociological Review* 80(2): 268–298.

Branco R and Costa E (2019) The golden age of tax expenditures: Fiscal welfare and inequality in Portugal (1989–2011). *New Political Economy* 24(6): 780–797.

Brautigam D, Fjeldstad O-H, and Moore M (2008) *Taxation and state-building in developing countries: Capacity and consent*. Cambridge University Press.

Bremer B and Bürgisser R (2025) Lower taxes at all costs? Evidence from a survey experiment in four European countries. *Journal of European Public Policy* 32(5): 1225–1252.

Brownlee WE (2003) *Funding the modern American state, 1941–1995*. Cambridge University Press.

Burman LE, Geissler C, and Toder EJ (2008) How big are total individual income tax expenditures, and who benefits from them? *American Economic Review* 98(2): 79–83.

Busemeyer MR, Garritzmann JL, Neimanns E, et al. (2018) Investing in education in Europe: Evidence from a new survey of public opinion. *Journal of European Social Policy* 28(1): 34–54.

Busemeyer MR, Garritzmann, JL, and Neimanns E (2020) *A loud but noisy signal?: Public opinion and education reform in Western Europe*. Cambridge University Press.

Busemeyer MR and Iversen T (2020) The welfare state with private alternatives: The transformation of popular support for social insurance. *The Journal of Politics* 82(2): 671–686.

Cameron DR (1978) The expansion of the public economy: A comparative analysis. *American Political Science Review* 72(4): 1243–1261.

Campbell, AL (2018) Tax designs and tax attitudes. *The Forum* 16(3): 369–397.

Campbell AL and Morgan KJ (2005) Financing the welfare state: Elite politics and the decline of the social insurance model in America. *Studies in American Political Development* 19(2): 173–195.

Campbell JL (1993) The state and fiscal sociology. *Annual Review of Sociology* 19(1): 163–185.

Cansunar A (2021) Who is high income, anyway? Social comparison, subjective group identification, and preferences over progressive taxation. *The Journal of Politics* 83(4): 1292–1306.

Carattini S, Carvalho M, and Fankhauser S (2018) Overcoming public resistance to carbon taxes. *Wiley Interdisciplinary Reviews: Climate Change* 9(5): e531.

Castles FG (1994) The wage earners' welfare state revisited: refurbishing the established model of Australian social protection, 1983–93. *Australian Journal of Social Issues* 29: 120–145. https://doi.org/10.1002/j.1839-4655.1994.tb00939.x

Cavaillé C (2023) *Fair enough?: Support for redistribution in the age of inequality.* Cambridge University Press.

Cichon M, Scholz W, Van De Meerendonk A, et al. (2004) *Financing social protection.* International Labour Organization.

Clasen J (2001) Social insurance and the contributory principle: A paradox in contemporary British social policy. *Social Policy & Administration* 35(6): 641–657.

Co-operation OfE and Development (2010) *Tax expenditures in OECD countries.* OECD.

Collier RB and Collier D (1991) *Shaping the political arena: Critical junctures, the labor movement, and regime dynamics in Latin America.* Princeton University Press.

Collins ML and Hughes G (2017) Supporting pension contributions through the tax system: Outcomes, costs and examining reform. *The Economic and Social Review* 48(4, Winter): 489–514.

Deacon B (2007) *Global social policy and governance.* Sage.

Donovan T and Bowler S (2022) Who wants to raise taxes? *Political Research Quarterly* 75(1): 35–46.

Döring H and Manow P (2017) Is proportional representation more favourable to the left? Electoral rules and their impact on elections, parliaments and the formation of cabinets. *British Journal of Political Science* 47(1): 149–164.

Downs A (1960) Why the government budget is too small in a democracy. *World Politics* 12(4): 541–563.

Ebbinghaus B (2011) *The varieties of pension governance: Pension privatization in Europe.* Oxford University Press.

Edlund J and Johansson Sevä I (2013) Exploring the "something for nothing" syndrome: Confused citizens or free riders? Evidence from Sweden. *Scandinavian Political Studies* 36(4): 293–319.

Einhorn RL (2009) Liberty, democracy, and capacity: Lessons from the early American tax regimes. In Martin IW, Mehrotra A and Prasad M (eds.) *The new fiscal sociology: Taxation in comparative and historical perspective.* Cambridge University Press, pp.155–172.

Elsässer L, Fastenrath F, Rehm M (2023) Making the rich pay? Social democracy and wealth taxation in Europe in the aftermath of the great financial crisis. *European Political Science Review* 15(2): 194–213.

Emmenegger P and Marx P (2019) The politics of inequality as organised spectacle: Why the Swiss do not want to tax the rich. *New Political Economy* 24(1): 103–124.

Enke B, Polborn M, and Wu A (2022) Morals as luxury goods and political polarization. September 30, 2022. Which we accessed on March 9, 2026: https://benjamin-enke.com/pdf/Morals_polarization.pdf.

Eriksen K and Fallan L (1996) Tax knowledge and attitudes towards taxation: A report on a quasi-experiment. *Journal of Economic Psychology* 17(3): 387–402.

Esping-Andersen G (1990) *The three worlds of welfare capitalism.* Princeton University Press.

Esping-Andersen G (1999) *Social foundations of postindustrial economies.* Oxford University Press.

Estevez-Abe M (2001) The forgotten link: The financial regulation of Japanese pension funds in comparative perspective. In Ebbinghaus B and Manow P (eds.) *Comparing welfare capitalism: Social policy and political economy in Europe, Japan and the USA.* Routledge, pp.190–216.

Faricy C and Ellis C (2014) Public attitudes toward social spending in the United States: The differences between direct spending and tax expenditures. *Political Behavior* 36: 53–76.

Faricy CG and Ellis C (2021) *The other side of the coin: Public opinion toward social tax expenditures.* Russell Sage Foundation.

Fastenrath F and Marx P (2023) The role of preference formation and perception in unequal representation. Combined evidence from elite interviews and focus groups in Germany. Working Paper No. 26.

Fastenrath F, Marx P, Truger A, et al. (2022) Why is it so difficult to tax the rich? Evidence from German policy-makers. *Journal of European Public Policy* 29(5): 767–786.

Fastenrath F, Schwan M, and Trampusch C (2017) Where states and markets meet: the financialisation of sovereign debt management. *New Political Economy* 22(3): 273–293.

Feldman N and Slemrod J (2009) War and taxation: When does patriotism overcome the free-rider impulse? In Martin IW, Mehrotra AK, and Prasad M. (eds.) *The new fiscal sociology: Taxation in comparative and historical perspective*. Cambridge University Press, pp. 138–154.

Fernández JJ and Jaime-Castillo AM (2018) The institutional foundation of social class differences in pro-redistribution attitudes: a cross-national analysis, 1985–2010. *Social Forces* 96(3): 1009–1038.

Fernández-Albertos J and Kuo A (2018) Income perception, information, and progressive taxation: Evidence from a survey experiment. *Political Science Research and Methods* 6(1): 83–110.

Finnegan JJ (2022) Institutions, climate change, and the foundations of long-term policymaking. *Comparative Political Studies* 55(7): 1198–1235.

Finseraas H (2012) Do Voters reward incumbent parties for reductions in tax burdens? An empirical analysis using Norwegian tax register data. *Journal of Elections, Public Opinion & Parties* 22(1): 95–108.

Fisman R, Jakiela P, and Kariv S (2015) How did distributional preferences change during the great recession? *Journal of Public Economics* 128: 84–95.

Flora P and Heidenheimer AJ (1981) *The development of welfare states in Europe and America*. Transaction Publishers.

Foucault M, Seki K, and Whitten GD (2017) Good times, bad times: Taxation and electoral accountability. *Electoral Studies* 45: 191–200.

Frankema E and Booth A (2020) *Fiscal capacity and the colonial state in Asia and Africa, c. 1850–1960*. Cambridge University Press.

Fuller GW (2015) Who's borrowing? Credit encouragement vs. credit mitigation in national financial systems. *Politics & Society* 43(2): 241–268.

Gale WG and Orszag PR (2004) Bush administration tax policy: Starving the beast? *Tax Notes* 105(8): 999–1002.

Ganghof S (2006) *The politics of income taxation: A comparative analysis*. ECPR Press.

Garcia-Muniesa J (2019) Economic crisis and support for progressive taxation in Europe. *European Societies* 21(2): 256–279.

Garritzmann JL, Neimanns E, and Busemeyer MR (2023) Public opinion towards welfare state reform: The role of political trust and government satisfaction. *European Journal of Political Research* 62(1): 197–220.

Genschel P (2002) Globalization, tax competition, and the welfare state. *Politics & Society* 30(2): 245–275.

Genschel P and Schwarz P (2011) Tax competition: A literature review. *Socio-Economic Review* 9(2): 339–370.

Genschel P and Seelkopf L (2021) *Global taxation: How modern taxes conquered the world*. Oxford University Press.

Geys B and Vermeir J (2008a) The political cost of taxation: New evidence from German popularity ratings. *Electoral Studies* 27(4): 633–648.

Geys B and Vermeir J (2008b) Taxation and presidential approval: separate effects from tax burden and tax structure turbulence? *Public Choice* 135(3–4): 301–317.

Gilbert N (2002) *Transformation of the welfare state: The silent surrender of public responsibility.* Oxford University Press.

Gilens M and Page BI (2014) Testing theories of American politics: Elites, interest groups, and average citizens. *Perspectives on Politics* 12(3): 564–581.

Gingrich J (2014) Visibility, values, and voters: The informational role of the welfare state. *The Journal of Politics* 76(2): 565–580.

Goldscheid R (1958 [1917]) A sociological approach to problems of public finance. In Musgrave RA and Peacock AT (eds.) *Classics in the theory of public finance.* Macmillan, pp. 202–213.

Goubin S, Jacques O, Kumlin S, et al. (2024) Why citizens want something for nothing: Three explanations for unfunded spending demand. *Scandinavian Political Studies* 49(1): e70034.

Green DP and Gerken AE (1989) Self-interest and public opinion toward smoking restrictions and cigarette taxes. *Public Opinion Quarterly* 53(1): 1–16.

Greve, B (1994) The hidden welfare state, tax expenditure and social policy: A comparative overview. *Scandinavian Journal of Social Welfare* 3: 203–211. https://doi.org/10.1111/j.1468-2397.1994.tb00227.x.

Guillaud E, Olckers M, and Zemmour M (2020) Four levers of redistribution: The impact of tax and transfer systems on inequality reduction. *Review of Income and Wealth* 66(2): 444–466.

Habibov N, Cheung A, and Auchynnikava A (2018) Does institutional trust increase willingness to pay more taxes to support the welfare state? *Sociological Spectrum* 38(1): 51–68.

Hacker JS (2002) *The divided welfare state: The battle over public and private social benefits in the United States.* Cambridge University Press.

Hacker JS (2004) Privatizing risk without privatizing the welfare state: The hidden politics of social policy retrenchment in the United States. *American Political Science Review* 98(2): 243–260.

Haffert L (2021a) Size and structure of the tax state in comparative perspective. In Hakelberg L and Seelkopf L (eds.) *Handbook on the politics of taxation.* Edward Elgar, pp. 98–112.

Haffert L (2021b) Tax policy as industrial policy in comparative capitalisms. *Journal of Economic Policy Reform* 24(4): 488–504.

Haffert L and Mertens D (2021) Between distribution and allocation: Growth models, sectoral coalitions and the politics of taxation revisited. *Socio-Economic Review* 19(2): 487–510.

Haffert L and Schulz DF (2020) Consumption taxation in the European Economic Community: fostering the common market or financing the welfare state? *JCMS: Journal of Common Market Studies* 58(2): 438–454.

Hall PA and Soskice D (2001) *Varieties of capitalism: The institutional foundations of comparative advantage*. Oxford University Press.

Hallerberg M and Basinger S (1998) Internationalization and changes in tax policy in OECD countries: The importance of domestic veto players. *Comparative Political Studies* 31(3): 321–352.

Hallerberg M and Von Hagen J (1997) *Electoral institutions, cabinet negotiations, and budget deficits in the European Union*. National Bureau of Economic Research Cambridge, MA.

Harris S (1941) *Economics of social security*. McGraw-Hill.

Hassel A, Naczyk M, and Wiß T (2019) *The political economy of pension financialisation: Public policy responses to the crisis*. Taylor & Francis.

Häusermann S (2006) Reform opportunities in a Bismarckian latecomer: Restructuring the Swiss welfare state. Paper presented at the Council of European Studies conference.

Hays JC (2009) *Globalization and the new politics of embedded liberalism*. Oxford University Press.

Helgason AF (2017) Unleashing the "money machine": the domestic political foundations of VAT adoption. *Socio-Economic Review* 15(4): 797–813.

Hertel-Fernandez A and Martin CJ (2018) How employers and conservatives shaped the modern tax state. In Huerlimann G, Brownlee WE and Ide E (eds.) *Worlds of taxation*. Springer International Publishing, pp. 17–48.

Hinrichs HH (1966) *A general theory of tax structure change during economic development*. Harvard Law School, Harvard University.

Hinrichs K (1997) *Social insurances and the culture of solidarity: The moral infrastructure of interpersonal redistributions-with special reference to the German health care system*. ZeS-Arbeitspapier.

Hinrichs K (2010) A social insurance state withers away. Welfare state reforms in Germany–or: attempts to turn around in a cul-de-sac. In Palier B (ed.) *A long goodbye to Bismarck? The politics of welfare reform in continental Europe*. Amsterdam University Press, pp. 45–72.

Hooghe M, Marien S, and De Vroome T (2012) The cognitive basis of trust. The relation between education, cognitive ability, and generalized and political trust. *Intelligence* 40(6): 604–613.

Hope D, Limberg J, and Weber N (2023) Why do (some) ordinary Americans support tax cuts for the rich? Evidence from a randomised survey experiment. *European Journal of Political Economy* 78: 102349.

Howard C (1997) *The hidden welfare state: Tax expenditures and social policy in the United States.* Princeton University Press.

Howard C (2021) *The welfare state nobody knows: Debunking myths about US social policy.* Princeton University Press.

Howard C (2023) *Who cares: The social safety net in America.* Oxford University Press.

Huo J (2021) Social democracy and the relative price of investment: Left governments, indirect taxation and the division of corporate income in affluent democracies. *Socio-Economic Review* 19(3): 953–974.

ILO (1984). *Financing social security: the options: an international analysis.* International Labour Office.

Immergut EM (1992) *Health politics: interests and institutions in Western Europe.* Cambridge University Press.

Iversen T and Soskice D (2006) Electoral institutions and the politics of coalitions: Why some democracies redistribute more than others. *American Political Science Review* 100(2): 165–181.

Jacobs AM (2011) *Governing for the long term: Democracy and the politics of investment.* Cambridge University Press.

Jacobs AM and Weaver RK (2015) When policies undo themselves: Self-undermining feedback as a source of policy change. *Governance* 28(4): 441–457.

Jacques O (2020) Funding the state: Taxation in Canada from a comparative politics perspective. In Heaman E and Tough D (eds.) *Who pays for Canada, taxation and fairness.* McGill Queen's University Press, pp. 37–65.

Jacques O (2023) Explaining willingness to pay taxes: The role of income, education, ideology. *Journal of European Social Policy* 33(3): 267–284.

Jacques O (2024) Welfare state regimes and social policy resistance to fiscal consolidations. *Social Policy & Administration* 58(5): 708–749.

Jacques O and Noël A (2018) The case for welfare state universalism, or the lasting relevance of the paradox of redistribution. *Journal of European Social Policy* 28(1): 70–85.

Jacques O and Weisstanner D (2022) The Micro-Foundations of Permanent Austerity: Income Stagnation and the Decline of Taxability in Advanced Democracies. LIS Working Paper Series, No. 839.

Johnson P, Lynch F, and Walker JG (2005) Income tax and elections in Britain, 1950–2001. *Electoral Studies* 24(3): 393–408.

Kangas O (2009) Pensions and pension funds in the making of a nation-state and a national economy: The case of Finland. In Hujo K and McClanahan S (eds.) *Financing social policy: Mobilizing resources for social development.* Palgrave Macmillan, pp. 246–263.

Kangas O and Palme J (2007) Social rights, structural needs and social expenditure: A comparative study of 18 OECD countries 1960–2000. In Clasen J and Siegel NA (eds.) *Investigating welfare state change: the "dependent variable problem" in comparative analysis.* Edward Elgar, pp. 106–132.

Karceski SM and Kiser E (2020) Is there a limit to the size of the state? The scope conditions of Wagner's law. *Journal of Institutional Economics* 16(2): 217–232.

Kato J (2003) *Regressive taxation and the welfare state: path dependence and policy diffusion.* Cambridge University Press.

Katzenstein PJ (1985) *Small states in world markets: Industrial policy in Europe.* Cornell University Press.

Kemmerling A (2009) *Taxing the working poor: The political origins and economic consequences of taxing low wages.* Edward Elgar.

Kemmerling A (2021) Social security contributions and the fiscal origins of the welfare state. In Genschel P and Seelkopf L (eds.) *Global taxation: How modern taxes conquered the world.* Oxford University Press, pp. 223–244.

Kemmerling A and Neugart M (2009) Financial market lobbies and pension reform. *European Journal of Political Economy* 25(2): 163–173.

King RF (2000) *Budgeting entitlements: The politics of food stamps.* Georgetown University Press.

Kiser E and Barzel Y (1991) The origins of democracy in England. *Rationality and Society* 3(4): 396–422.

Kiser E and Karceski SM (2017) Political economy of taxation. *Annual Review of Political Science* 20(1): 75–92.

Klein J (2004) The politics of economic security: Employee benefits and the privatization of New Deal liberalism. *Journal of Policy History* 16(1): 34–65.

Klitgaard MB and Elmelund-Præstekær C (2014) The partisanship of systemic retrenchment: Tax policy and welfare reform in Denmark 1975–2008. *European Political Science Review* 6(1): 1–19.

Koreh M (2017) The political economy of social insurance: Towards a fiscal-centred framework. *Social Policy & Administration* 51(1): 114–132.

Koreh M and Béland D (2017) Reconsidering the fiscal–social policy nexus: the case of social insurance. *Policy & Politics* 45(2): 271–286.

Koreh M and Mandelkern R (2023) Trade-offs of government credibility institutions: market credibility vs. social credibility. *Journal of European Public* Policy 31(11): 3539–3560.

Koreh M and Shalev M (2017) Pathways to neoliberalism. In Maron A and Shalev M (eds.) *Neoliberalism as a State Project: Changing the Political Economy of Israel*. Oxford University Press, pp. 93–113.

Koreh M, Zemmour M, and Palier B (2024) The hidden transformation of social insurance: Making contributory finance progressive. In *Paper presented at the CES Conference*, July 3–5, Lyon.

Korpi W and Palme J (1998) The paradox of redistribution and strategies of equality: Welfare state institutions, inequality, and poverty in the Western countries. *American Sociological Review*: 63(5): 661–687.

Lachapelle E, Bergeron T, Nadeau R, et al. (2021) Citizens' willingness to support new taxes for COVID-19 measures and the role of trust. *Politics & Policy* 49(3): 534–565.

Leff HM (1983) Taxing the "forgotten Man": The politics of social security finance in the new deal. *Journal of American History* 70(2): 359–379.

Levi M (1988) *Of rule and revenue*. University of California Press.

Levi M (1989) *Of rule and revenue*. University of California Press.

Lierse H (2022) Globalization and the societal consensus of wealth tax cuts. *Journal of European Public Policy* 29(5): 748–766.

Lijphart A (2012) *Patterns of democracy: Government forms and performance in thirty-six countries*. Yale University Press.

Limberg J (2020) What's fair? Preferences for tax progressivity in the wake of the financial crisis. *Journal of Public Policy* 40(2): 171–193.

Lindert PH (2004) *Growing public: Volume 1, the story: Social spending and economic growth since the eighteenth century*. Cambridge University Press.

Lindh A (2015) Public opinion against markets? Attitudes towards market distribution of social services–A comparison of 17 countries. *Social Policy & Administration*, 49(7): 887–910.

Mahler VA and Jesuit DK (2006) Fiscal redistribution in the developed countries: New insights from the Luxembourg Income Study. *Socio-Economic Review* 4(3): 483–511.

Maman D (2021) State financial interests and changes in investment behavior of institutional investors: The case of financial market development in Israel. *Socio-Economic Review* 20(4): 2073–2093.

Manow P (2004) Federalism and the welfare state: The German case. *Working papers of the ZeS* 8: 175–200.

Manow P (2010) Trajectories of fiscal adjustment in Bismarckian welfare systems. In Palier B (ed.) *A long goodbye to Bismarck? The politics of welfare reform in continental Europe*. Amsterdam University Press, pp. 279–299.

Manow P and Seils E (2000) Adjusting badly: The German welfare state, structural change, and the open economy. *Welfare and Work in the Open Economy* 2, 264–307.

Martin CJ (2015) Labour market coordination and the evolution of tax regimes. *Socio-Economic Review* 13(1): 33–54.

Martin I and Prasad M (2014) Taxes and fiscal sociology. *Annual Review of Sociology* 40: 331–345.

Martin IW, Mehrotra AK, and Prasad M (2009) The thunder of history: The origins and development of the new fiscal sociology. In Martin IW, Mehrotra AK, and Prasad M (eds.) *The New Fiscal Sociology: Taxation in Comparative and Historical Perspective*. Cambridge University Press, pp. 1–27.

Martin WI and Gabay N (2018) Tax policy and tax protest in 20 rich democracies, 1980–2010. *The British Journal of Sociology* 69(3): 647–669.

Mathisen R (2021) Taxing the 1 per cent: Public Opinion vs Public Policy. *British Journal of Political Science* 54(3): 595–611.

McDaniel C (2007) Average tax rates on consumption, investment, labor and capital in the OECD 1950–2003. *Manuscript, Arizona State University* 19602004.

Mehrotra AK (2016) "From contested concept to cornerstone of administrative practice": Social learning and the early history of US tax withholding. *Columbia Journal of Tax Law* 7: 144.

Meltzer AH and Richard SF (1981) A rational theory of the size of government. *Journal of Political Economy* 89(5): 914–927.

Mettler S (2011) *The submerged state: How invisible government policies undermine American democracy*. University of Chicago Press.

Mettler S (2018) *The government-citizen disconnect*. Russell Sage Foundation.

Montanari I (2001) Modernization, globalization and the welfare state: A comparative analysis of old and new convergence of social insurance since 1930. *The British Journal of Sociology* 52(3): 469–494.

Moore M, Prichard W and Fjeldstad OH (2018) *Taxing Africa: Coercion, reform and development*. Bloomsbury Academic.

Morel N (2025) *The politics of fiscal welfare: Towards a social division of welfare and labour*. Policy Press.

Morel N and Palme J (2018) Financing the welfare state and the politics of taxation. In Greve B (ed.) *Routledge handbook of the welfare state*. Routledge, pp. 467–476.

Morel N, Touzet C, and Zemmour M (2018) Fiscal welfare in Europe: Why should we care and what do we know so far? *Journal of European Social Policy* 28(5): 549–560.

Morel N, Touzet C, and Zemmour M (2019) From the hidden welfare state to the hidden part of welfare state reform: Analyzing the uses and effects of fiscal welfare in France. *Social Policy & Administration* 53(1): 34–48.

Morgan JK (2005) Financing the Welfare State: US Tax Politics in Comparative Perspective. Unpublished Manuscript, Department of Political Science, George Washington University.

Morgan K and Prasad M (2009) The origins of tax systems: A French–American comparison. *The American Journal of Sociology* 114(5): 1350–1394.

Morrison KM (2015) *Nontaxation and representation*. Cambridge University Press.

Musgrave RA and Musgrave PB (1973) *Public finance in theory and practice*. McGraw-Hill.

Myles J and Quadagno J (2002) Political theories of the welfare state. *Social Service Review* 76(1): 34–57.

Naczyk M and Palier B (2014) Feed the beast: Finance capitalism and the spread of pension privatisation in Europe. *SSRN 2551521*.

North DC (1993) Institutions and credible commitment. *Journal of Institutional and Theoretical Economics (JITE)/Zeitschrift für die gesamte Staatswissenschaft* 149(1): 11–23.

North DC and Weingast BR (1989) Constitutions and commitment: the evolution of institutions governing public choice in seventeenth-century England. *The Journal of Economic History* 49(04): 803–832.

Obinger H, Petersen K, and Starke P (2018) Introduction: Studying the warfare-welfare nexus. In Obinger H, Petersen K and Starke P (eds.) *Warfare and welfare: Military conflict and welfare state development in Western countries*. Oxford University Press, pp. 1–35.

OECD (1998) *Harmful tax competition: an emerging global issue*. OECD Publishing

OECD (2007) *Tax Administration in OECD and Selected Non-OECD Countries: Comparative Information Series (2006)*. Paris: OECD Publishing|.

OECD (2010) *Tax expenditures in OECD countries*. OECD Publishing. https://www.oecd.org/content/dam/oecd/en/publications/reports/2010/01/tax-expenditures-in-oecd-countries_g1ghbcaf/9789264076907-en.pdf.

OECD (2018) *Income redistribution across OECD countries: Main findings and policy implications* (OECD Economic Policy Paper No. 23).

OECD (2023) *Social expenditures dataset*. OECD.

Okunogbe O and Santoro F (2023) Increasing tax collection in African countries: The role of information technology. *Journal of African Economies* 32 (Supplement_1): i57–i83.

Orenstein MA (2013) Pension privatization: The transnational campaign. In Kott S and Droux J (eds.) *Globalizing social rights: The International Labour Organization and beyond*. Palgrave Macmillan, pp. 280–292.

Palier B (2010) *A long goodbye to Bismarck?: The politics of welfare reform in continental Europe*. Amsterdam University Press.

Palme J, Nelson K, Sjöberg O, and Minas R (2009) *European social models, protection and inclusion*. Institute for Future Studies.

Papadia A and Truchlewski Z (2021) Plucking the goose while it's hissing: Recessions and tax introductions. In Genschel P and Seelkopf L (eds.) *Global taxation: How modern taxes conquered the world*. Oxford University Press.

Park G (2011) *Spending without taxation: FILP and the politics of public finance in Japan*. Stanford University Press.

Pavolini E, Jessoula M, and Natili M (2024) The political economy of fiscal welfare. In Greve B, Moreira A, and van Gerven M (eds.) *Handbook on the political economy of social policy*. Edward Elgar, pp. 141–152.

Peacock AT and Wiseman J (1961) The growth of public expenditure in the United Kingdom. In *The growth of public expenditure in the United Kingdom*. Princeton University Press, pp. 32–30.

Pierson P (1994) *Dismantling the welfare state?: Reagan, Thatcher and the politics of retrenchment*. Cambridge University Press.

Pierson, P (1996) The new politics of the welfare state. *World Politics*, 48(2): 143–179.

Pierson P (1998) Irresistible forces, immovable objects: Post-industrial welfare states confront permanent austerity. *Journal of European Public Policy* 5(4): 539–560.

Pierson P (2000) Increasing returns, path dependence, and the study of politics. *American Political Science Review* 94(2): 251–267.

Pierson P (2001) Coping with permanent austerity: Welfare state retrenchment in affluent democracies. In Pierson P (ed.) *The new politics of the welfare state*. Oxford University Press, pp. 410–456.

Platt L (2021) What is social policy? International, interdisciplinary and applied. *The London School of Economics and Political Science*.

Pontusson J (2005) *Inequality and prosperity: Social Europe vs. liberal America*. Cornell University Press.

Prasad M and Deng Y (2009) Taxation and the worlds of welfare. *Socio-Economic Review* 7(3): 431–457.

Provencher Y, Godbout L, and St-Cerny S (2022) Social tax expenditures in Quebec (Canada): The state of play. *International Journal of Social Welfare* 31(2): 225–235.

Przeworski A and Wallerstein M (1988) Structural dependence of the state on capital. *American Political Science Review* 82(1): 11–29.

Rodrik D (1998) Why do more open economies have bigger governments? *Journal of Political Economy* 106(5): 997–1032.

Rogan M (2022) Taxation and the informal sector in the global South: Strengthening the social contract without reciprocity? In Alfers L, Chen M and Plagerson S (eds.) *Social contracts and informal workers in the Global South*. Edward Elgar, pp. 85–105.

Ruane S, Collins ML, and Sinfield A (2020) The centrality of taxation to social policy. *Social Policy and Society* 19(3): 437–453.

Russell KL (2018) The politics of hidden policy: Feedback effects and the charitable contributions deduction. *Politics & Society* 46(1): 53–80.

Sachweh P (2016) Social justice and the welfare state: Institutions, outcomes, and attitudes in comparative perspective. In Sabbagh C and Schmitt M (eds.) *Handbook of social justice theory and research*. Springer, 293–313.

San Juan EA (2017) Who pays the price of civilization? *Columbia Journal of Tax Law* 9: 45.

Scheve K and Stasavage D (2016) *Taxing the rich: A history of fiscal fairness in the United States and Europe*. Princeton University Press.

Scheve K and Stasavage D (2023) Equal treatment and the inelasticity of tax policy to rising inequality. *Comparative Political Studies* 56(4): 435–464.

Schmitt C, Lierse H, and Obinger H (2020) Funding social protection: Mapping and explaining welfare state financing in a global perspective. *Global Social Policy* 20(2): 143–164.

Schumpeter JA (1991 [1918]) The crisis of the tax state. In Swedberg R (ed.) *The economics and sociology of capitalism*. Princeton University Press, pp. 99–140.

Seelkopf L, Lierse H, and Schmitt C (2016) Trade liberalization and the global expansion of modern taxes. *Review of International Political Economy* 23(2): 208–231.

Sinfield A (2020) Building social policies in fiscal welfare. *Social Policy and Society* 19(3): 487–499.

Sinfield A (2023) Fiscal welfare and tax expenditures. In Lymer A, May M and Sinfield A (eds.) *Taxation and social policy*. Policy Press, pp.46–66.

Sinn S (1992) The taming of Leviathan: competition among governments. *Constitutional Political Economy* 3(2): 177–196.

Sjoberg O (2000) *Duties in the welfare state: Working and paying for social rights*. Swedish Institute for Social Research.

Spencer H (1897) *The principles of sociology*. D. Appleton.

Stanley L and Hartman TK (2018) Tax preferences, fiscal transparency, and the meaning of welfare: An experimental study. *Political Studies* 66(4): 830–850.

Stantcheva S (2021) Understanding tax policy: How do people reason? *The Quarterly Journal of Economics* 136(4): 2309–2369.

Stebbing A and Spies-Butcher B (2010) Universal welfare by 'other means'? Social tax expenditures and the Australian dual welfare state. *Journal of Social Policy* 39(4): 585–606.

Steinmo S (1993) *Taxation and democracy: Swedish, British, and American approaches to financing the modern state*. Yale University Press.

Steinmo S (1994) The end of redistribution? International pressures and domestic tax policy choices. *Challenge* 37(6): 9–17.

Steinmo S (2003) The evolution of policy ideas: Tax policy in the 20th century. *The British Journal of Politics & International Relations* 5(2): 206–236.

Steuerle CE (1992) *The tax decade: How taxes came to dominate the public agenda*. The Urban Insitute.

Steuerle CE (1996) Financing the American state at the turn of the century. In Brownlee WE (ed.) *Funding the modern American State, 1941–1995: The Rise and fall of the era of easy finance*. Cambridge University Press, pp. 409–444.

Stiers D, Hooghe M, Goubin S, et al. (2021) Support for progressive taxation: self-interest (rightly understood), ideology, and political sophistication. *Journal of European Public Policy* 9(4): 550–567.

Streeck W (2014) *Buying time: The delayed crisis of democratic capitalism*. Verso Books.

Sumino T (2016) Level or concentration? A cross-national analysis of public attitudes towards taxation policies. *Social Indicators Research* 129(3): 1115–1134.

Surrey SS (1973) *Pathways to tax reform: the concept of tax expenditures*. Harvard University Press.

Swedberg R (1991) *The economics and sociology of capitalism: Joseph A. Schumpeter*. Princeton University Press.

Tillman ER and Park B (2009) Do voters reward and punish governments for changes in income taxes? *Journal of Elections, Public Opinion and Parties* 19(3): 313–331.

Tilly C (1992) *Coercion, capital, and European states, AD 990–1992*. Wiley-Blackwell.

Tilly C (2009) Extraction and democracy. In Martin IW, Prasad M and Mehrotra A (eds.) *The new fiscal sociology: Taxation in comparative and historical perspective*. Cambridge University Press, pp.173–182.

Timmons JF (2005) The fiscal contract: States, taxes, and public services. *World Politics* 57(4): 530–567.

Timmons JF (2010) Taxation and credible commitment: Left, right, and partisan turnover. *Comparative Politics* 42(2): 207–227.

Titmuss R (2019) *Essays on the welfare state (reissue)*. Policy Press.

Trampusch C (2018) A State-centred explanation of the finance-pension nexus: New Zealand's pension reforms as a typical case. *Social Policy & Administration* 52(1): 343–364.

Truchlewski Z (2020) "Oh, what a tangled web we weave": How tax linkages shape responsiveness in the United Kingdom and France. *Party Politics* 26(3): 280–290.

Tuxhorn KL, D'Attoma J and Steinmo S (2021) Do citizens want something for nothing? Mass attitudes and the federal budget. *Politics & Policy* 49(3): 566–593.

van Berkel HHA (2010) The provision of income protection and activation services for the unemployed in "active" welfare states: An international comparison. *Journal of Social Policy* 39(1): 17–34.

van Ganzen B (2023) Determinants of top personal income tax rates in 19 OECD countries, 1981–2018. *Journal of Public Policy* 43(3): 401–426.

Van Oorschot W (2006) Making the difference in social Europe: Deservingness perceptions among citizens of European welfare states. *Journal of European Social Policy* 16(1): 23–42.

Vlandas T, Jacques O, and Weisstanner D (2024) Economic Decline and the Political Backlash against Advanced Welfare States. Working Paper, the Swiss Political Science Association Conference in St Gallen in February 2024.

Wagner N (2012) Financing social security in the EU: Business as usual? *International Labour Review* 151(4): 333–349.

Wang A (2017) Patience as the rational foundation of sociotropic voting. *Electoral Studies* 50: 15–25.

Wang C and Caminada K (2011) Disentangling income inequality and the redistributive effect of social transfers and taxes in 36 LIS countries. *Department of Economics Research Memorandum*: 1–53. https://papers.ssrn.com/sol3/papers.cfm?abstract_id=1909941.

White J (2015) Entitlement budgeting vs. Bureau budgeting. In Rubin IS (ed.) *Public budgeting*. Routledge, pp. 334–348.

Wilensky HL (1974) *The welfare state and equality: Structural and ideological roots of public expenditures*. University of California Press.

Wilensky LH (2002) *Rich democracies: Political economy, public policy, and performance*. University of California Press.

Williamson V (2017) *Read my lips: Why Americans are proud to pay taxes*. Princeton University Press.

Zhu L and Lipsmeyer CS (2015) Policy feedback and economic risk: The influence of privatization on social policy preferences. *Journal of European Public Policy* 22(10): 1489–1511.

Acknowledgements

This Element is the product of close collaboration among the three authors. Michal Koreh took the lead on drafting Sections 2 and 3, and Olivier Jacques on Sections 4 and 5. Daniel Béland authored the Introduction and Conclusion (Sections 1 and 6), and made important contributions to Section 2. All three authors revised the manuscript together. The authors thank the participants in the PEN (Political Economy of Neoliberalism) workshop at Tel Aviv University, Alexandra Hays-Alberstat, and the anonymous reviewers for their comments and suggestions. The authors also thank Leo Ahrens, Lukas Haffert, and Zbigniew Truchlewski for sharing their research. The authors are grateful to the editors of the series for their support. Finally, Michal Koreh acknowledges support from the Israel Science Foundation: Grant Number 1934/18.

Cambridge Elements

Public Policy

M. Ramesh
National University of Singapore (NUS)

M Ramesh is UNESCO Chair on Social Policy Design at the Lee Kuan Yew School of Public Policy, NUS. His research focuses on governance and social policy in East and Southeast Asia, in addition to public policy institutions and processes. He has published extensively in reputed international journals. He is co-editor of *Policy and Society* and *Policy Design and Practice*.

Michael Howlett
Simon Fraser University, British Columbia

Michael Howlett is Burnaby Mountain Professor and Canada Research Chair (Tier1) in the Department of Political Science, Simon Fraser University. He specialises in public policy analysis, and resource and environmental policy. He is currently editor-in-chief of *Policy Sciences* and co-editor of the *Journal of Comparative Policy Analysis, Policy and Society* and *Policy Design and Practice*.

Xun WU
Hong Kong University of Science and Technology (Guangzhou)

Xun WU is currently a Professor at the Innovation, Policy and Entrepreneurship Thrust at the Society Hub of Hong Kong University of Science and Technology (Guangzhou). He is a policy scientist with a strong interest in the linkage between policy analysis and public management. Trained in engineering, economics, public administration, and policy analysis, his research seeks to make contribution to the design of effective public policies in dealing emerging policy challenges across Asian countries.

Judith Clifton
University of Cantabria

Judith Clifton is Professor of Economics at the University of Cantabria, Spain, and Editor-in-Chief of *Journal of Economic Policy Reform*. Her research interests include the determinants and consequences of public policy across a wide range of public services, from infrastructure to health, particularly in Europe and Latin America, as well as public banks, especially, the European Investment Bank. Most recently, she is principal investigator on the Horizon Europe Project GREENPATHS (www.greenpaths.info) on the just green transition.

Eduardo Araral
National University of Singapore (NUS)

Eduardo Araral specializes in the study of the causes and consequences of institutions for collective action and the governance of the commons. He is widely published in various journals and books and has presented in more than ninety conferences. Ed was a 2021–22 Fellow at the Center for Advanced Study of Behavioral Sciences, Stanford University. He has received more than US$6.6 million in external research grants as the lead or co-PI for public agencies and corporations. He currently serves as a Special Issue Editor (collective action, commons, institutions, governance) for World Development and is a member of the editorial boards of *Water Economics and Policy*, *World Development Sustainability*, *Water Alternatives* and the *International Journal of the Commons*.

About the Series

Elements in Public Policy is a concise and authoritative collection of assessments of the state of the art and future research directions in public policy research, as well as substantive new research on key topics. Edited by leading scholars in the field, the series is an ideal medium for reflecting on and advancing the understanding of critical issues in the public sphere. Collectively, the series provides a forum for broad and diverse coverage of all major topics in the field while integrating different disciplinary and methodological approaches.

Cambridge Elements

Public Policy

Elements in the Series

Relationality: The Inner Life of Public Policy
Raul P. Lejano and Wing Shan Kan

Understanding Accountability in Democratic Governance
Yannis Papadopoulos

Public Inquiries and Policy Design
Alastair Stark and Sophie Yates

Multiple Streams and Policy Ambiguity
Rob A. DeLeo, Reimut Zohlnhöfer and Nikolaos Zahariadis

Designing Behavioural Insights for Policy: Processes, Capacities & Institutions
Ishani Mukherjee and Assel Mussagulova

Robust Governance in Turbulent Times
Christopher Ansell, Eva Sørensen, Jacob Torfing and Jarle Trondal

Symbolic Policy
Laurie Boussaguet and Florence Faucher

Policy Entrepreneurs, Crises, and Policy Change
Evangelia Petridou, Jörgen Sparf, Nikolaos Zahariadis and Thomas Birkland

Public Contracting for Social Outcomes
Clare J FitzGerald and Ruairi Macdonald

Bad Public Policy: Malignity, Volatility, and the Inherent Vices of Policy-Making
Michael Howlett, Ching Leong and Tim Legrand

Artificial Intelligence and Public Policy
Fernando Filgueiras

Taxation and Social Policy: Financing the Welfare State
Michal Koreh, Olivier Jacques and Daniel Béland

A full series listing is available at: www.cambridge.org/EPPO

For EU product safety concerns, contact us at Calle de José Abascal, 56–1°,
28003 Madrid, Spain or eugpsr@cambridge.org.